A Social Market Economy and European Economic Monetary Union

Dario Velo & Francesco Velo

A Social Market Economy and European Economic Monetary Union

PETER LANG
Bern · Berlin · Bruxelles · Frankfurt am Main · New York · Oxford · Wien

Bibliographic information published by die Deutsche Nationalbibliothek
Die Deutsche Nationalbibliothek lists this publication in the Deutsche Nationalbibliografie; detailed bibliographic data is available on the Internet at ‹http://dnb.d-nb.de›.

British Library Cataloguing-in-Publication Data: A catalogue record for this book is available from The British Library, Great Britain

Library of Congress Cataloging-in-Publication Data

Velo, Dario.
A social market economy and European economic monetary union /
Dario Velo & Francesco Velo.
pages cm
Includes bibliographical references.
ISBN 978-3-0343-1291-2
1. Europe–Economic integration. 2. Monetary unions–Europe. 3. European Union countries–Economic conditions. 4. European Union. I. Velo, Francesco. II. Title.
HC241.V395 2013
337.1'42–dc23
2013026686

This publication has been funded with support from the European Commission. This publication reflects the views of the Authors, and the Commission cannot be held responsible for any use which may be made of the information contained therein.

Cover illustration: Klingelhöferstraße 14, Berlin, by Dario Velo.

ISBN 978-3-0343-1291-2 pb. ISBN 978-3-0351-0625-1 eBook

Contents

Summary

Europe is on the threshold of a new stage in the integration process involving a transition from monetary union to economic union. As has always happened in its history, progress in integration confronts Europe with the need to guarantee the continuity of this process as well as the discontinuity arising from solutions found for the new problems.

Economic union will impose on Europeans the task of deciding how to orient the system at both an economic level and a social one, as well as establishing the constitutional rules required for managing increased interdependency. The European Union has a chance to address in a new way a problem present since its birth. This involves "What Europe" it intends to be, what kind of society, what economy, what form of statehood it will adopt and with which constituent values. A social market economy is the starting point for addressing these issues.

Europe and the world are now facing one another with two opposing visions containing a series of forces and ideas.

A first perspective asserted itself in the last part of the 20th century and resulted in globalisation, radical liberism (markets without institutions) and relativism.

A second perspective is appearing now as a convergence of new ideals, and includes a new humanism, a social market economy, neoliberalism (orderly relations between the state and markets), human rights, federalism and subsidiarity.

European economic union could represent the historicising of this second ideal vision and Europe may be the place where a new economic, social and state order is developed.

A social market economy could then be perceived as the model on the basis of which Christian and secular-liberal traditions may find common ground and together shape a free, supportive Europe, open to a historical project.

Rules are called upon to guarantee the orderly development of this new Europe. Monetary union has already approved rules aimed at guaranteeing the management of inflation and state deficits while respecting subsidiarity. Economic union will be called upon to develop this approach extending it to sovereign debt and means for development.

Zero inflation, zero deficit and zero debt and new instruments for development are the long-term objectives for orienting economic-monetary unification towards good governance.

In this perspective, one strategic problem in Europe's future consists of relations with the United States.

Both federations are faced with similar problems; a crisis experienced by the old order, a need to decide "which" new order is needed. The starting points for the U.S. and Europe are different, but the development path may be a shared one.

Preface

Faced with the complexity of the current crisis experienced in a new manner by western countries within the globalisation process, I believe this book provides a significant contribution both to an understanding of the mechanisms at the basis of these events and in proposing prospects for its positive evolution.

The economic and social model inherited by the 20th century is without doubt experiencing a profound crisis that demands the humility and wisdom of a radical reconsideration.

The events of recent years have proved all the limitations of a paradigm based on the solipsistic exaltation of the individual regardless of his constitutive belonging to a community.

As Pope Benedict XVI specified in *Caritas in veritate* (Nos. 22 and 35), this system has not only created inequalities, and therefore also ultimately inflicted crushing damage at a social level, but the lack of internal forms of solidarity and loyalty have prevented the market itself from implementing its economic function that, in order to act positively, should regulate itself not on the basis of commutative justice but also on the basis of distributive and social fairness. The lack of attention paid to these values has encouraged dishonest behaviour that corrodes reciprocal trust, and the seriousness of the loss of credibility is there for all to see.

This book has the courage to propose a different path, in search of a shared model, while also contributing to recreate public ethics as an alternative to individualism.

It is interesting that, going against the trend compared to so many current publications now oriented towards considering the Pacific area as crucial, this attempt is made still trusting in Europe. With its history and current possible prospects, Europe appears as the privileged context in which the crisis could be addressed in an incisive and innovative manner, before other continents.

By searching for new opportunities in order to create a fairer society, the authors create a dialogue between the objectives of European economic-monetary union and those of a European social market economy; an intense exchange between a scientific-economic approach and one based on values and ethics.

In doing this the authors choose not to linger on references to current affairs or the technical aspects of possible solutions, but rather to keep attention focused on the crisis' profound origins, on the nature of the choices to be made and on the fundamental characteristics of the new order that may arise from the current recession.

According to this analysis, by developing the experience of a social market economy matured in Germany and in core-Europe, Europe – and in a different way also the United States – could become the favourable context in which to observe the passage from a model of globalisation marked by radical liberism and a postmodern relativism of values, to a new order respecting fundamental human rights, organised according to criteria of subsidiarity and solidarity, and one promoting through a social market economy, a different liberism capable of respectful relations between the state and the market.

This is a new form of humanism, the characteristics of which are very similar to the teachings of the Social Doctrine of the Church.

The authors are aware of this convergence between the Social Doctrine of the Church and a social market economy, especially on key values such as freedom, solidarity and subsidiarity; the social market economy was historically defined on the basis of merging secular traditions and the principles of the Christian social doctrine, both Catholic and Protestant.

It is interesting to observe how the book attempts to historicise these guiding principles, addressing what progress may be possible nowadays in Europe, in order to pave the way for further developments at a global level, also through the hoped-for Atlantic social market economy that a renewed axis between the Old Continent and the United States could promote.

Regardless of whether this solution is feasible or not, one must acknowledge that the authors have not only well-understood that the current situation requires new solutions, but also the courage to present a specific one, that is not so much an "adaptation" of the existing economic model, as literature for this sector so often continues to present, but a radical change of paradigm moving in the direction indicated by Benedict XVI when in his aforementioned Encyclical (No. 37), he expressed the hope for solutions in which, "the canons of justice must be respected from the outset, as the economic process unfolds, and not just afterwards or incidentally."

I therefore hope that this book will contribute effectively to the current debate among those who, in all honesty caring about the fate of a better future in the *city of humankind*, will not restrict themselves to "dealing with daily matters" but will envisage and cultivate "long-term solutions" that characterised the wise founding fathers of the European Union.

Francesco Card. Coccopalmerio
President of Pontificium Consilium de Legum Textibus

Chapter I. Lessons from the past: Monetary Union

1.1 The innovative characteristics of the European unification process

The European unification process has developed through a series of phases following a basically consistent logic. Every phase has been characterised by a central problem to be resolved as the condition for the process' advancement and one that was the specific object of the alternative strategic options considered[1]. Each phase followed a basically similar development logic. Each phase began with a crisis, arising from a problem that had arisen, but had not yet been resolved, and experiencing a moment of decisive importance when the specific objective to be pursued in order to adequately address the issue was identified. This was followed by a transition phase, which was more or less long depending on the importance and the difficulties of the transformation being implemented, gradually achieving the objective pursued[2].

One characteristic of the European unification process is the importance assumed by the development of a material constituent process, which, once the necessary conditions were achieved, resulted in a formal constitutional solution sealing the progress achieved[3].

---

1 Monnet, J., *Mémoires*, Fayard, Paris, 1976; Albertini, M., *Il federalismo*, Il Mulino, Bologna, 1986.

2 Melchionni, M.G., *Altiero Spinelli et Jean Monnet*, Fondation Jean Monnet pour l'Europe, Lausanne, 1993.

3 This characteristic assumed by the European unification process does not correspond to the vision of those who have perceived this process as a repetition of the unification of the United States. Spinelli, A., Rossi, E., *Il Manifesto di Ventotene*, Guida, Naples, 1982.

Progress made on the basis of successive phases, and the role played by the material constituent process interacted, thereby contributing to making the European unification process an innovative one equipped with flexibility. The result has been the gradual creation of a form of statehood founded on a number of fundamental guiding principles and values and not on traditional historically experimented models.

This aforementioned aspect can be clarified by comparing the European and the American experience[4]. Ever since it was established as an independent state, the United States has been equipped with a constitution, a federal government, an army and a currency[5].

United States constitutional order has experienced continuous evolution, with changes that have modified the initial balance. The constitution written by the Founding Fathers was a firm reference point and guaranteed continuity within the historical development process.

The European experience has been symmetrically the opposite. The Old Continent identified the constitution as the objective to be achieved after a long process and gradually created a governing framework, originally merging solutions that are traditionally considered as alternatives of a confederal or federal kind[6]. At the moment this process is still undergoing a developmental phase half a century after it began. The outcome has been a series of juridical, economic and social consequences. Implications of a constitutional nature emerged with the greatest clarity as a direct result of the fact that the entire process has been addressed at gradually creating a new kind of statehood, not always following a linear logic.

---

4 On this subject see the single edition of *The European Union Review* on European-United States relations. *The European Union Review*, 1-2/10.

5 Hamilton, A., Madison, J., Jay, J., *The Federalist*, McLean, New York, 1788.

6 Majocchi, L.V., *La difficile costruzione dell'unità europea*, Jaca Book, Milan, 1996.

In the absence of a formal constitution and a consolidated government, in the traditional sense of the word, the integration process has achieved a transferral of power and competences from a national to a European level, attributing them at times to a European *government* and at times to European *governance,* but not to a pre-established and stable institutional order.

When it became more important, the transferral of power set out a chapter of the future constitution which has become characterised in terms of a progressive sequence of partial achievements. An emblematic example of this process has been the creation of Monetary Union with the setting up of the European Central Bank and the ratification of the Maastricht Treaty[7].

One problem that has characterised the integration process throughout its implementation consists in the fact that it found itself in the condition of gradually drafting a coherent constitution, without being able to rely on an *ex-ante* definition of the constitutional framework that is the objective of the process itself. So as to find this coherence, decisions involving constitutional matters were able to refer to the founding characteristics of the integration process and to the values that have supported it: freedom, solidarity and subsidiarity[8]. These values determine "a large span net" that leaves ample space for the various choices deemed necessary to define the implementation of whatever issue is being debated.

As mentioned, the European legislative process could not be based on the certainties made available to United States legislators, who were able to refer to an organic constitution at the basis of the country's historical development.

---

7 Padoa-Schioppa, T., *La lunga via per l'Euro*, Il Mulino, Bologna, 2004.

8 These are the values of a social market economy which represented the meeting point of the great European, secular and Christian, political and spiritual traditions. See Forte, F., Felice F. (edited by), *Il liberalismo delle regole. Genesi ed eredità dell'economia sociale di mercato*, Rubbettino, Rome, 2010.

The relative constitutional indeterminateness with which Europeans have had to coexist can be perceived as a strength or a weakness depending on the idea of statehood one has.

A large span net is perceived as a weakness for those referring to a traditional model for a strong and centralised state as the objective Europe must aim for[9]. On the other hand, this same large span net is perceived as a strength for those considering the integration process as a workshop for defining a new model of state, a new relationship between society, the economy and the state[10].

For those who share this innovative vision, the European Union is a historical opportunity for founding a state of law in the most complete sense, a state therefore in which the law is the basis of internal order and of the role played at an international level in a manner never previously experienced[11].

---

9 Spinelli, A., *Come ho tentato di diventare saggio*, Il Mulino, Bologna, 2006.

10 Hirsch, E., *Ainsi va la vie*, Fondation Jean Monnet pour l'Europe, Lausanne, 1988.

11 Zamagni, S. (a cura di), *Economia, democrazia, istituzioni in una società in trasformazione*, Il Mulino, Bologna, 1997.

1.2 New European statehood tested by the crisis: the beginning of Economic-Monetary Union

The integration process started in a favourable context with America's highly evolutionary leadership over Europe and more in general over the western world, albeit characterised by significant elements. The United States incentivised the very birth of the integration process, supporting it at a political and economic level.

It is thus sufficient to bear in mind how the United States conditioned the allocation of the Marshall Plan's aid to its being managed jointly by European countries. This choice is emblematic in order to perceive the very essence of relations between Europe and the United States in the immediate post-war period[12].

European statehood was able to develop gradually because monetary, financial, commercial and defence order was ensured by the United States in a stable manner and in ways that encouraged integration[13].

Within this framework, 1968 marked a breakaway moment, obliging Europe to autonomously assume direct responsibilities in addressing the international economic-political crisis. The fragility of European institutions emerged very clearly when faced with the seriousness of the crisis they were suddenly called-upon to address[14].

---

12 In truth this strategic choice can be dated back to the years of the war, during which President Roosevelt played a personal role in supporting forces in favour of European integration. On this subject see Monnet, J., *Mémoires*, op. cit.; Cordier, D., *J. Moulin*, Vol. I, II, III, Lattés, Paris, various years.

13 Preda, D., *Storia di una speranza. La battaglia per la CED e la federazione europea*, Jaca Book, Milan, 1990.

14 A brief reconstruction of this stage in European integration can be found in Velo, D., *La crisi economica internazionale e l'alternativa europea*, Giuffrè, Milan, 1976.

The lessons that can be learned from an analysis of the crisis that began in 1968 are of a general nature. Contingent issues that had to be addressed led to the adoption of instantly operational measures to tackle the most serious emergencies. What is more important, is that the crisis opened a debate on adequate strategies needed to provide an effective long-term alternative.

The positions that were gradually outlined can be summarised as being based on three fundamental alternatives. A first alternative consisted of options with more clearly conservative characteristics and, ultimately, this category includes analyses and interventions addressed at consolidating the existing order and more specifically at reiterating the centrality of the American currency as the mainstay for the international monetary system[15].

A second alternative with radical characteristics was that presented by those supporting the need to address this crisis with European constitutional reform. In their opinion this was the only way of equipping Europe with the means to effectively deal with the crisis and hence a government, a currency and economic policies[16].

A third alternative was inspired by Monnet's ideas and consisted of those who supported the possibility of creating economic-monetary union, albeit in the absence of a European government in the traditional sense of the word. This alternative envisaged the possibility of setting up a central bank and a currency, thereby implementing progress of a constitutional nature in the integration process, using the juridical instruments previously used in stages already completed by the Union. Ultimately, a new treaty[17].

---

15 Magnifico. G., *Euro: squilibri finanziari e spiragli di soluzione*, Luiss University Press, Rome, 2008.

16 Paolini, E., *Altiero Spinelli. Appunti per una biografia*, Il Mulino, Bologna, 1988.

17 Jozzo, A., Velo, D., "L'autonomia della banca centrale in Italia e in Europa", in *Moneta e Credito*, 134/81.

It was this third alternative that would be adopted by Pierre Werner and would lead the monetary unification process all the way to the founding of the ECB[18].

It is evident how *ex-post* this third alternative is easily identifiable as the expression of continuity, while respecting the fundamental innovative characteristics of the unification process. It is also evident how *ex-ante* it was hard to envisage that it would be possible to address the crisis experienced by the international monetary system and create a currency capable of achieving the same stature as the U.S. dollar in the absence of a real government.

New European statehood emerged victorious from the international monetary system's crisis, achieving Monetary Union, activating a gradual process to transfer monetary sovereignty from a national to a European level and implementing a series of intermediate solutions capable of addressing a series of monetary crises.

The second alternative mentioned above, one of a federalist radical nature, was based on the idea that it was necessary to address the international monetary crisis from its very roots with a final and immediate solution[19].

The Monnet approach, at the basis of new European statehood, has instead tried to develop a process capable of acquiring rising consensus and of gradually becoming stronger.

This activated a process of later correlated events. Just as European unification proceeded in stages, so did Monetary Union within

18 Louis, J.V. (edited by), *Vers un système européen de banques centrales*, Université libre de Bruxelles, Brussels, 1989.

19 This was the approach always adopted by Altiero Spinelli throughout his life, bearing witness to the ultimate objective regardless of failures blamed specifically on his radicalism. Preda, D., "First attempts to found an European Federal State: a retrospective glance", *The European Union Review*, 1/99.

the European integration, until the founding of the European Central Bank was achieved[20].

This process is of great importance within the framework of this analysis, and is a precedent capable of clarifying matters in order to understand ongoing developments in the unification process. Due to the importance of the lessons learned, it seems best to analyse in greater detail the experiences involving European monetary unification.

1.3 Lessons learned from European Monetary Union

The European Central Bank (ECB) was created at the end of a lengthy process. The manner in which the ECB was created is significant for understanding the European model of a federal central bank and for assessing its impact on the future development of Economic-Monetary Union. Coherently with the more general integration process, Monetary Union can be better understood by referring to the manner in which the monetary sovereignty of member states was transferred to the integration process. It is restrictive to analyse Monetary Union as a stable and definitive solution. Analysing the Euro-system as a not yet completed process is a perspective that actually allows one to understand in greater depth the manner in which the system currently operates, which is profoundly influenced by its nature as an institution that is still undergoing change[21].

---

20 It is legitimate to ask oneself whether Monetary Union is still an incomplete process. Thus the creation of the ECB could be considered as a stage, albeit one of crucial importance, in a process still open to additional progress. Velo, D., *La neutralizzazione della moneta e del debito pubblico e la centralità della politica fiscale. Il modello europeo in divenire*, currently being published.

21 It is here that one can identify the root of the differences between the European System of Central Banks (ESCB) and the American Federal Reserve System, di-

The fundamental aspect that unites the integration process, as a whole, and the process involving monetary unification within it, consists of the gradual transferral of powers, when consensus for this transferral emerged in order to manage problems that matured.

The greatest difficulty has been the identification of a specific problem that requires addressing. The Monnet approach has always been concerned with searching for the point on which pressure could be applied to move forward with the integration process[22].

Defining solutions for resolving problems identified in this manner is an extremely important moment and experience acquired also confirms that the definition of solutions has a technical aspect that facilitates their management[23].

After the crisis of the international monetary system founded in Bretton Woods, with the Werner plan Europe set itself the objective of achieving Economic-Monetary Union. Establishing the objective and starting to draft a plan for achieving the objective was a historical moment. Furthermore, at the time there were not yet the conditions for implementing a first significant transferral of powers at a monetary level from the states to the Union.

Faced with the crisis of the international monetary system that started in 1968, the German mark was the only currency capable of providing a stable alternative. It became the nucleus around which other currencies aggregated, but these were currencies that did not share the same capacity to remain linked to the German one. The Mark Area was created by the ensemble of currencies with the greatest capacity to maintain stable relations over time, referring to the

---

rectly linked to differences between European and United States statehood. This aspect was perceived by the Monnet school of thought when faced with the problem of defining coherence between Monetary Union and the European constitutional structure. Maillet, P., "Quelle organisation monétaire dans une Europe élargie a géométrie variable organisée?", *The European Union Review*, 1/96.

22 Monnet, J., *Memoires*, op. cit.

23 Velo D. (a cura di), *L'autonomia della Banca Centrale*, Cacucci, Bari, 1995.

German mark as the linchpin currency. This solution seemed instantly applicable since it required no transfer of sovereignty nor the organisation of new institutions. This solution simultaneously drew strength from the project for European Monetary Union which provided a reference framework and allowed the Mark Area to be perceived as the initial phase of a more general and open project capable of also receiving the approval of countries not yet participating[24].

The Mark Area resulted in the creation of the European Monetary System (EMS) thus assuming more clearly the characteristics of a European answer to the international monetary crisis. The EMS succeeded thanks to an alliance between France and Germany, which became the basis for the system's power, equipping it with stability and guaranteeing the necessary conditions for the adhesion of the currencies of other European countries.

These two leader countries should be acknowledged with the merit of having approved the creation of a European monetary institution that would be responsible for the management of the EMS, which started the transferral of monetary sovereignty to the integration process. This marked the beginning of the process that would result in the creation of the ECB.

The EMS took shape as an inter-governmental agreement of a confederal nature[25]. Its credibility derived from the guaranteed support of a core-Europe, from the correspondence between the objectives pursued and the government instruments activated, from its organic position within the community's institutional framework, guaranteeing respect of the general interest.

One fundamental aspect guaranteeing the development of the European Monetary System consisted in the system's capacity to in-

---

24 Louis, J.V., *L'Union Européenne et sa monnaie*, Université Libre de Bruxelles, Brussels, 2009.

25 Maillet, P., Velo D., *Europe à géometrie variable, transition vers l'intégration*, L'Harmattan, Paris, 1994.

fluence national policies, orienting them in a European direction. This result seems all the more important if one considers that the EMS has only been able to rely on confederal means of governance[26]. This success can be correctly assessed by returning the analysis of how the EMS works to the more general process in which it is situated. It was this process that has supported a series of initiatives that increased consensus on monetary unification, without necessarily affecting the EMS' specific functionality[27].

In this manner the EMS was able to establish the basic conditions needed for later progress in the monetary unification process. This phase of progressive convergence allowed for a broad debate that once again opposed the supporters of radical unification solutions, the supporters of confederal solutions orientated at stabilising the existing order and the supporters of united solutions founded on constitutional gradualism[28]. At the centre of this debate was the problem of the rules that would regulate European monetary order. Initially, thanks to the initiatives taken by just a few[29], then increasingly clearly in a more shared manner, the possibility of having fiscal policies as a means for governing the economy while 'neutralising' monetary and financial policy, was outlined. This last point directly questioned sovereign debt. A change in this sense was inevitably initially greeted with widespread scepticism since it changed governing instruments imposing a profound reorganisation of national state apparatus.

Regardless of the contingencies and the transition required to implement necessary changes, the unavoidable option consisted in the constitutional order that the creation of a central European bank would

---

26 AA.VV., "The evolution of economic governance in EMU", *Economic Papers* n. 328, European Commission, Brussels, 2008.

27 Reference to the private use of the ECU and the issuing of bonds in this European 'currency' should be addressed in this sense. Jozzo, A. (editor), *The international monetary system and economic recovery*, Thema, Turin, 1979.

28 Gros, D., Thygesen, N., *European monetary integration*, Longman, London, 1992.

29 Jozzo A., Velo D., "L'autonomia della banca centrale in Italia e in Europa", op. cit.

have contributed to defining. The crucial node was the ECB's autonomy *versus* its dependence on a defined governing power.

The transition from the EMS to Monetary Union, in the real sense of the word, would more specifically involve the assumption of a shared vision of three very important issues.

Firstly, it was necessary to discuss the possibility of creating a European Central Bank with the participation of a limited number of countries with the agreement of countries not initially participating, allowing them the possibility to fully join Monetary Union at a later date[30].

Secondly, a problem of decisive importance was the drafting of rules for managing the European Central Bank that would guarantee respect for the competences of member states.

Thirdly and lastly, Monetary Union imposed the need to guarantee coherent behaviour by member countries, in particular as far as government spending was concerned.

These three problems translated into real terms the aforementioned more general problem of a constitutional nature. The definition of juridical acts required the pinpointing of decisions with the three problems briefly summarised here corresponding to the three fundamental juridical steps taken which allowed Monetary Union to be achieved[31].

---

30 AA.VV., *La cooperazione rafforzata e l'Unione Economica*, Giuffrè, Milan, 2007.

31 Commission for the Study of Economic and Monetary Union (Delors Report), *Report on Economic and Monetary Union in the European Community*, European Commission, Luxembourg, 1989.

1.4 The rules of Monetary Union: enhanced cooperation

The first of the aforementioned problems that had to be regulated in a specific manner consisted in the possibility of creating Monetary Union for a number of countries inferior to those belonging to the European Union.

From the very beginning, the integration process developed thanks to initiatives taken by a number of countries which assumed responsibility for guiding the process. In order to start and strengthen the integration process, Europe was divided between the founding countries, initially with the six countries that signed the Treaties of Rome on one hand, and on the other those that adopted a 'wait and see' strategy. The identification of the six founding member states was the result of a process started with the founding of the European Coal and Steel Community (ECSC). In order to achieve this first founding act in the integration process, France and Germany had stated their readiness to proceed autonomously with a number of member states that were fewer than those who eventually joined[32].

The success achieved by the integration process has modified the balance. The rising number of countries joining the Union posed the problem of institutionally outlining guidelines for the initiative role undertaken by some countries, acknowledging the possibility of implementing achievements that would only at a later date be adhered to by all member countries. This problem was posed with the greatest clarity and urgency when central-eastern European countries joined the European Union following the disintegration of the Soviet Union.

Enhanced cooperation was the answer provided to these problems. This form of integration was achieved gradually. With the Nice Treaty a mature framework was provided, although de facto solutions

---

32 Melchionni, M.G., "Charles de Gaulle and Jean Monnet: two differing strategies for Europe", *The European Union Review*, 3/00.

had been previously developed that can be perceived as early forms of enhanced cooperation[33]. The Lisbon Treaty establishes the option of developing forms of structured cooperation, which can be interpreted as a further development on the path to enhanced cooperation. The renewal of institutional solutions in order to manage emerging problems, and for which the solutions created in previous phases are at least to a certain extent inadequate, is a fundamental characteristic of the European unification process[34].

The possibility of creating Monetary Union for a number of countries inferior in number to that of European Union member states is set within such a context. Furthermore, the importance of this decision imposed a rigorous solution in order to create a stable reference point for the later development of this Monetary Union. Having reached the goal of creating a single currency, potentially a global means for payments and reserves, the juridical basis could not be restricted to the capacity to support the beginning of a process, but needed to also guarantee the regulation of future events. Never before had such a complex issue required addressing[35].

The solution adopted to allow the creation of what would become known as the "eurozone" was *de facto* a rigorous form of enhanced cooperation. This terminology was never used in the course of the de-

33 Maillet, P., "Un modéle de governance Européen favorable à l'apparition d'une politique diversifiée et cordonnée", *The European Union Review*, 1-2/01.

34 To better understand the European unification process, one fundamental lesson of this doctrine is the inversion achieved in relations between the institutions and the process. In the well-established states institutions are a stable reference point, while processes involving change develop within them. In the European experience, continuity can be more easily identified with the process, while the institutions called upon to govern it change within it. See Albertini, M., *Il Federalismo*, op. cit.

35 To achieve this, an emblematic case was the development of a European industrial policy, which was founded upon a series of achievements based on the principles of enhanced cooperation with a logic involving gradually increased cooperation. Velo, D. (edited by), *L'Europa dei progetti*, Giuffrè, Milan, 2007.

cision-making process that resulted in the creation of the European Central Bank. The procedure adopted widely preceded the Nice Treaty. This level of coherence cannot be considered as a coincidence and the author believes it is legitimate to believe that the players were fully aware of this during the decision-making process[36].

Fundamentally the rules for Monetary Union were approved by all member states, even those postponing a decision to join the eurozone. These countries were acknowledged the right to join the Monetary Union at a later date, on condition they had the necessary requirements but without needing the approval of the many countries already members of the eurozone.

1.5 The rules of Monetary Union: the right of seigniorage and the stability of the currency's value

The second fundamental problem to be faced consisted of the transferral of sovereignty conceded by the states to the Union linked to the creation of the European currency. The extent of the sovereignty transferred depended partly on the creation of the ECB, and partly on the manner in which the ECB was to operate. It was immediately clear that there was a widespread awareness that this second aspect could have played a predominant role[37].

36 From this perspective it is not particularly important to address the problem of whether Monetary Union anticipated the Nice Treaty, predicting its content that was at the time already being debated, or vice versa whether the Nice Treaty took into account the debate that had developed within the monetary unification process. What is important is the convergence of the decision-making processes; this observation is related to the method of the analysis developed here.

37 During the debate that developed in Europe in setting up Monetary Union, an evocative image of this issue was proposed so as to clarify the object of the debate also for a public with a limited economic culture. This image can be summarised

From the perspective of member states, the creation of the ECB generated the risk of an uncontrollable transferral of sovereignty. Should the ECB have been organised following the model used for central banks in centralised national states, it would have been a means for draining resources in favour of European institutions creating a monetary base, all the more to the extent it could have caused inflation.

In order to protect themselves from such a risk, the only possible practical solution for member states was to regulate the ECB's workability and organisation with provisions of a constitutional nature. The solution was found in defining a federal charter for the ECB and in imposing the defence of monetary stability as a constraint.

The ECB was recognised as an independent institution, protected in its autonomy and at the same time restricted in its activities. The right of seigniorage was therefore neutralised as a means for financing European or national institutions. The experience acquired in the first ten years of the ECB's existence confirms that the seigniorage has self-financed the bank's capital allowing it to play its role according to the logic of strict orthodoxy[38].

One must emphasize the interaction between the organisational aspects and the constraints imposed on the ECB's scope of operations in order to organically ensure the bank's placement within the European constitutional order. The drafting of the ECB's charter respected the fundamental values of European constitutional order thereby contributing to strengthening this order by confirming it.

---

as follows; when one equips armed forces with weapons one must define the rules of engagement. It is fundamental to know if, when and how the forces are permitted to use them. Thus the right to coin money must be qualified in terms of the use of this power, with and without inflationist effects. The author of this efficiently educational image was the great economist Robert Triffin, who did not however use it in his papers and books.

38 On this see the periodical bulletins and annual reports published by the ECB itself.

The ECB is organised in a federal manner and this obliges its central bodies to ensure they have the consensus of central banks belonging to the system through a structured consultation process. This consultation is extended to national state powers called upon to support the economic government enacted by the ECB itself.

Responsibility for controlling the financial markets and the banking system has remained the competence of national authorities. One can envisage that these aspects will be regulated in a different manner only when the European Union addresses the objective of Economic Union.

The European Commission has been precluded from intervening in the ECB's management, thereby making it directly or indirectly a means of government. It is instead compulsory for the president of the ECB to present a report to the European Parliament in order to answer for his work and specifically respect for the charter commitment to guarantee monetary stability.

This organisation has allowed the ECB to operate autonomously and to pursue its charter's objective to defend the value of the currency. The fact that the ECB cannot fund state authorities has in turn restricted their interest in interfering with the ECB's management. This has resulted in the activation of a virtuous circuit that has contributed to increase the Central Bank's authority and its capacity to operate effectively.

The only important and unresolved risk, and one that could not be resolved when the ECB was founded, derives from the fact that it marked the forward frontier of integration in the economic sector. This *per se* exposed the ECB to the risk of being called upon to play a substitute role, filling in power vacuums not yet resolved by the integration process. Ultimately, this was the risk that Monetary Union might not quickly be followed by Economic Union. Such a possibility emerged in concrete form in 2011 with the international economic crisis.

1.6 The rules of Monetary Union: Maastricht and the constraints placed to sovereign debt and to budget deficits

The objective assigned by statute to the ECB to guarantee the value of the currency set in motion the 'neutralisation' of monetary policy as an instrument of economic policy. This marked a radical change for some member states, which had traditionally resorted to monetary policy as their main form of intervention for influencing the economic system. These countries found themselves obliged to renew their means of governing the economy, replacing monetary policy with fiscal policy and adopting a federal model as the alternative to the traditional bureaucratic-centralised operational logic. The difficulties posed by this task resulted in an awareness of the need to expect a reasonably long transition period during which the national instruments for economic governance would gradually be reorganised.

The problems posed by this task became immediately appeared to be even broader since the direct implication of the objective of guaranteeing stability to the value of the currency arose from the need to limit all resorting to deficit spending and to indebtedness by state authorities at all levels, both national and international. The neutralisation of monetary policy posed the problem of neutralising financial policy, resulting in increasingly privileging fiscal policy as the fundamental basis of economic policy. The extent of this transformation was so broad that it made it all the more difficult for operators trained with a traditional economic culture to fully assess the implications of the changes made. The problems also emerged at a cultural level and the generation of economists formed in the Keynesian school of thought were obliged to confront the need to critically review the founding conceptual rules at the basis of their culture[39].

39 Kuhn emphasised how the changing of the dominant theoretical perspectives presents an even greater problem than the one met by men of action involved in

The Maastricht Treaty posed a number of fundamental rules for the development of Economic-Monetary Union, in particular coherently orienting the development of monetary, financial and fiscal policy. In this manner a process was started and the established rules were attributed the value of guidelines for managing a lengthy transition period. The rigorous drafting of rules destined to guaranteeing the governing of Monetary-Economic union, *in primis* the precise definition of multilevel European fiscal federalism, was postponed to the phase involving the creation of fully implemented Economic Union. Relations between monetary, financial and fiscal policies were based, at least in this initial phase, on a gradual convergence of three parallel tracks[40], consisting of the management of the currency, debt and the budget.

One crucial aspect in assessing the measures adopted by the Maastricht Treaty is the fact that only some member countries of the European Union have joined the Eurozone. It is equally important that the countries that did join the Eurozone had profoundly different basic economic conditions. When monetary union was implemented, core-Europe presented profoundly different economic-financial equilibriums compared to countries in southern Europe[41].

---

modifying economic-social equilibriums. Kuhn, T., *La struttura delle rivoluzioni scientifiche*, ed. it. Einaudi, Turin, 1968.

40 The image of a convergence of parallel tracks includes *per se* the hypothesis of a change in the original order so as to overcome the contradiction contained in the image. This expression resumes the historical-political analysis elaborated by A. Moro when referring to the Italian experience. The allusion is to the only apparently imaginative expression "parallel convergences" coined by the eminent Italian jurist and statesman.

41 Over the years that followed, experience proved the validity of some of the ideas that guided the initial definition of Monetary Union. These considerations are not an assessment of the measures adopted in terms of effectiveness, efficiency and fairness. On this subject see Maillet, P., "Un modéle de governance européen, favorable à l'apparition d'une politique diversifiée et cordonnée", op. cit.

A constitutional choice, coherently oriented towards the founding principles of European integration was also made in the financial, fiscal and monetary sectors. The subsidiarity principle, as previously mentioned, is the European Union's main founding principle. It requires that fiscal power and the possibility to resort to debt and deficit be distributed at various levels following rules that guarantee a balance between resources and competences. This is essential in order to prevent one institutional level discretionally appropriating itself of resources prevaricating over other institutional levels[42].

The federal distribution of fiscal power and of the possibility of deficit spending as well as resorting to sovereign debt, added to the neutralisation of monetary policy, are complementary means for disciplining expenditure capacity at every single level of the Union. One can understand how the constraints imposed to achieve this objective were not rigidly established when the process was launched. The neutralisation of monetary policy imposed a profound reorganisation of the state apparatus in Eurozone countries. This reorganisation would have been difficult to implement should it have been necessary to simultaneously neutralise financial policies and radically modify the possibility of generating a budget deficit.

The decision concerning the possibility of generating a budget deficit and resorting to sovereign debt should be regulated or perhaps even abolished was therefore postponed to the phase involving Economic Union following a significantly long transition period.

In order to assess the rules implemented by the Maastricht Treaty, it can be helpful to refer to the precedent established by the regulation of the European budget. The Maastricht Treaty can be interpreted from this point of view as the beginning of the extension to all institutional levels of the rules regulating the community's budget.

---

42 Louit, C., "Fédéralism fiscal: l'expérience française d'après Maastricht", *The European Union Review*, 3/97.

At a European level rigid constraints have been established as well as precise and rigorous procedures for regulating expenditure capacity and taxation. The European Commission is not permitted to get into debt. The Union's budget can be modified only following the same procedures with which the Treaties were signed and this is an acknowledgement of the constitutional nature of the allocation of fiscal power[43].

At a national level, the Maastricht Treaty has restricted the freedom of the deficit spending and indebtedness of public administrations establishing parameters and constraints as well as sanctions if such parameters are not respected.

These parameters should be interpreted in the light of the situation that existed when they were defined. They are a reference point for the process involving the homogenisation of the macro-economic equilibriums of the nations that joined. At a local and regional level, these guidelines are destined to gradually take root, following a "waterfall" development and it is difficult to envisage that member states could accept different rules at a national or local level that would privilege them. Should this occur, the burden of adjustment would fall only upon the national level, *de facto* equally restricting the possibility of playing an innovative role in the governing of the country[44].

At a monetary level, stability has been guaranteed by attributing broad autonomy to the ECB and binding its action to respect for the priority objective of protecting the currency's value. This order has become part of the European Union's constitutional heritage.

A corresponding solution was never achieved at a fiscal level. In previous pages, Monetary Union has been described as 'works in pro-

43 Rideau, J., *Union Européenne. Commentaire des Traités modifiés par le Traité de Nice*, LGDJ, Paris, 2001.

44 Lamfalussy, A., "Macro-coordination of fiscal policies in an Economic and Monetary Union in Europe", in AA.VV. *Report on Economic and Monetary Union in the European Community*, Office for official publications of the European Communities, Luxembourg, 1988.

gress'. Such an observation is even more appropriately applicable to fiscal policy, directly linked to the delay concerning Economic Union compared to Monetary Union within the framework of the unification process.

The constraint on deficit spending at a fiscal level and the one to state debt at a financial level were extended from the European level, at which these principles were already rigorously applied, to a national level with the Maastricht Treaty, albeit with margins of flexibility. It is clear that member states would have encountered serious problems if they had, over the short-term, renounced this degree of discretionality.

One cannot exclude the opposite hypothesis of an inversion of tendency with the extension at a European level of the possibility, which nowadays characterises member states, of resorting to debt and to deficit spending. This alternative is one of constitutional importance and to be correctly understood must be set within the fundamental characteristics of the unification process. This alternative questions the very nature of European statehood, paving the way for a redefinition of the European Union according to the more traditional models of centralised-bureaucratic states.

The extent of this alternative leads one to estimate that it is unlikely it will be resolved over the short term[45].

The Maastricht Treaty can be renegotiated and not necessarily in evolutionary terms.

When envisaging the development of Maastricht in evolutionary terms, as an element of Economic Union, it becomes realistic to envisage a two-phase process. Economic Union requires the rigorous establishment of relations between monetary policy, sovereign debt, and fiscal policy. Fiscal federalism is destined to become the framework

45 At a European level this problem is influenced by international relations; it has an international dimension in a broader and more long term perspective. See Velo, F., "Fiscal federalism: from the Gramm-Rudman-Hollings Act to the Atlantic Maastricht Treaty", *The European Union Review*, 1-2/10.

within which the governing of the economy is destined to be organised. This order is the objective to be defined and will certainly require an adequate transition period. It is thus imaginable that in order to manage the transition there will be the need for measures destined to progressively lose their importance when all member countries approach the conditions established when Economic Union is achieved. Transitional measures will be necessary to accompany the process involving the re-entry of the more deviant countries. This is a possibility that has already emerged at the first signs of the economic crisis even as this book is being written[46].

The unification process involving the monetary aspect lasted three decades before the ECB was founded and a first nucleus of European Union member countries renounced monetary sovereignty. In the fiscal and financial sectors the unification process is destined to take a period of time and one cannot predict whether it will be long or short. In the fiscal and financial sectors the process involving European convergence is already gradually taking place, through an oriented but not largely yet defined process. If the federal logic which has characterised the European unification process throughout its implementation should be confirmed, the convergence between monetary, fiscal and financial policies will be inevitable, with a reallocation over time of power in order to ensure that the federal order itself becomes increasingly more coherent and effective[47].

The Maastricht Treaty is a bridge between Monetary Union and Economic Union. If one considers past experience, the Treaty allowed the launching of Monetary Union, establishing a European regulation of state expenditure. If one considers the prospects of Economic Union, the Treaty is an acquired element capable of influencing future

---

46 This book was written between 2010 and 2012. The chapter above was written in the spring of 2011.

47 Artis, M., Nixon, F. (eds), *The Economics of the European Union*, Oxford University Press, Oxford, 2007.

choices some of which it already contains *in nuce*. The experience acquired over the years through the application of provisions contained in the treaty is a source of lessons to be drawn on in defining the rules for Economic Union.

Chapter II. Future challenges: Economic Union and a Social Market Economy

2.1 From Monetary Union to Economic Union: continuity and discontinuity in the unification process

In the interpretation outlined in the previous chapter, the Maastricht Treaty can be considered as the *trait d'union* between Monetary Union and Economic Union. The Treaty has made the implementation of Monetary Union possible, envisaging a number of budget and sovereign debt policies that can be considered a starting point for defining the rules of Economic Union.

The Maastricht Treaty permitted the launching of the phase known as Monetary Union and set the premise for the beginning of the next phase, Economic Union. The Treaty is initially linked to monetary unification since it was from this treaty that it came into being, and, considering Maastricht as a preview of Economic Union is an interpretation that requires verification and is certainly not yet widely shared.

The Maastricht Treaty can also be perceived as a moment of continuity between Monetary Union and Economic Union from another perspective. The continuity characterizing the very logic of the unification process means that the experience acquired in the course of the monetary unification process has a high chance of setting a precedent able to orient ideas and initiatives for understanding and resolving problems that will emerge in the course of the development of Economic Union. As previously mentioned, Monetary Union was achieved after a series of stages that permitted the implementation of progressive development. Economic Union could repeat that experience by being implemented in various phases before achieving the objective pursued. In this context, the Maastricht Treaty established rules that could be developed further on the basis of a gradual logic involving progress by phases.

These considerations take one back to Pierre Werner's founding project. To the extent that Economic-Monetary Union is a common project, it is legitimate to expect that the players and the applicable alternatives will be comparable, both when referring to the initial phase of Monetary Union, and when referring to the following phase involving Economic Union.

The process's continuity should not lead one to underestimate aspects of discontinuity. Implementing Economic Union implies the adoption of broader measures compared to those set out in the Maastricht Treaty and not necessarily homogeneous ones. Continuity in processes is supported by the constitutional dimension of Monetary and Economic Union, while discontinuity arises from specific issues that must be addressed and the practical solutions required.

Identifying the key issues within such complexity is an extremely difficult task and one that is exposed to great risks of making mistakes. It is also the exercise sine qua non understanding and influencing processes cannot be achieved[48].

We have already seen in previous pages how these considerations are applied to the European monetary unification process. In the three decades between the Werner Plan and the introduction of the euro, the crises, analyses, projects and measures adopted amounted to an immensely vast ensemble of events[49]. The fundamental choices that al-

---

48 Identifying the key issues is an exercise distinguishing those who assume responsibility; this is an element in the creation of what is new. Innovation is based on understanding. This is a border separating innovation from utopia, not comparable at least in the short-term to the commitment involved in implementation. See examples of this orientation set out by Triffin, R., *Gold and the Dollar Crisis*, Yale University Press, New Haven, 1960.

49 This ensemble has a historical value and includes experiences the lessons of which will fuel reflection for a long period of time. As far as analysis is con-

lowed for the development of the monetary unification process resulted in a far smaller sub-group within this vast archive of knowledge. It is up to scholars to rediscover and understand ex-post the link between the problems that were more difficult to resolve and the strategies that allowed them to be addressed in an evolutionary manner and finally to overcome them. It was up to the players of the process to undertake this same exercise, ex-ante[50]. The same applies to scholars who have assumed the responsibility of contributing to the process, as they must adventure into the insidious land of the unknown.

Applying this approach to Economic Union results in looking for the fundamental problems that will have to be addressed in the process, the solution of which will be required in order to complete this new phase in the unification process.

The basis on which our analysis in the pages that follow is founded, is that Economic Union poses two fundamental problems. A first problem is posed by the very substance of Economic Union, while a second one consists of the rules to be implemented to ensure an orderly development of such a union.

The substance of Monetary Union was clear from the very beginning and alluded to the creation of a single currency and a European central bank. A problem of fundamental importance was posed by the drafting of the rules that Monetary Union would be called upon to respect.

Economic Union poses a very broad ranging series of issues that will not necessarily be part of an agreement. A brief list of some of the possible contents is sufficient for understanding the complexity of the next stage in European unification. The problems to be addressed in-

---

cerned complexity provides a fertile environment. Papadia, F., "Unione Economica e Monetaria dopo Maastricht", *Il Mulino*, 339/92.

50 Allow me to pay homage to a maestro from the Pavia school of thought, Riccardo Argenziano, who liked to repeat a maxim by a famous French philosopher to clarify his own opinion regards to life and philosophy: "think like a man of action, act like a man of thought." The problem with this maxim lies in its implementation.

clude relations between the economy and society, relations between society and the state, the division of roles between the state and the market, welfare reform, the issue of sustainable development and the need to reorganise production processes in order to ensure they respect the environment. This list is not a complete one but it does indicate the significance of Economic Union.

Monetary Union has called into question relations between national and European institutions. The rules established for a European governing of the currency have been of the utmost importance and have been able to orient public authorities at a European and national level towards the objective of good governance.

Economic Union will result in a new relationship between national institutions responsible for the economy and European institutions. The rules for Economic Union have resulted in a debate concerning social order and relations between society, the markets and the state.

Economic Union does not only put up for discussion a European governing of the economy, but also the issues on which such government would be called upon to act. Very briefly, Economic Union requires the designation of an economic-social model capable of obtaining the necessary consensus of citizens.

The Lisbon Treaty has already outlined a project that could have this value; this project is a social market economy. This reference is broadly indeterminate; it is known how a social market economy came into being in core-Europe. It must now be fully defined at a European level with the approval of all Europeans, while taking into account the different experiences of member states.

It will only be possible for the Economic Union project to address the issue of rules after having defined its contents in greater detail.

2.2. European social market economy

Social market economy has its roots in the continent's centuries-old history and in the experiences matured in core-Europe after World War II. European social market economy as the basis for Economic Union implies overcoming the economic aspect in order to set it within the framework of social-economic and institutional order. Such an enlargement results in a higher level of difficulties and complexities and also corresponds to the ongoing evolution in developed countries and is thus an inescapable fact[51].

The roots of social order are very profound in all systems. Social order can only change slowly and the main player in such change is society itself. Adding the social dimension to our analysis results in the reconstruction of the historical process that saw the birth and success of early experiences of social market economy becoming all the more important.

This form of analysis results in a perception of a social market economy, not as an ideology, but as an order with its history set in a specific context, the determination of which must be analysed.

---

51 French culture has traditionally resorted to the publication of pamphlets in order to encourage philosophical-political reflection on ongoing changes. As a recent example of this tradition see the pamphlet by Hessel, S., *Indignez vous!*, Indigene, Montpellier, 2011.

2.3 The origins of the social market economy

Over the centuries Europe has developed its own economic and social model based on freedom and solidarity. When comparing the European experience to that of other countries, it clearly emerges how there is a European specificity that is deeply-rooted in our centuries-old history.

The European model came into being gradually through a development process that was not always linear. In the various historical phases, freedom and solidarity were present in different manners and the same applies when considering the experiences in the various regions in Europe.

The first formulation of an economic-social and institutional order ascribable to contemporary forms of social market economy can be found in the writings of W. Rathenau, first published in 1916. Rathenau's "The New Economy" appeared at a crucial moment in Germany's history. In the middle of the war, the country's emerging managerial class reflected on the end of a historical cycle and the future that awaited Germany and Europe at the end of the conflict. The old leadership had the merit of developing industrialisation, but according to Rathenau it had exhausted its innovative capabilities[52].

Just before World War I and parallel to Rathenau's ideas, Luigi Einaudi wrote a famous article in which he outlined two possible scenarios for Europe: an evolutionary scenario, consisting of federal unification, and a regressive one involving a new hegemonic attempt by a more powerful state, which at the time was Germany. Einaudi understood how the second scenario implied a destructive war[53].

---

52 Rathenau, W., *L'economia nuova*, ed. it. Einaudi, Turin, 1976.

53 For a more complete overview of the analysis concerning Einaudi's ideas see: Einaudi, L., *La guerra e l'unità europea*, Comunità, Milan, 1950; Einaudi, L., *Lo scrittoio del Presidente*, Einaudi, Turin, 1956.

The analyses presented by Einaudi and Rathenau are converging. From different intellectual perspectives they posed the same problems. How could a new statehood and new economic-social order be established that would correspond to the potential expressed by European society? The intuition of these two great economists would guide European reconstruction in the second half of the century following World War II.

Economic Union confirms the convergence between Einaudi and Rathenau's ideas. The analysis that follows is largely based on the interpretative hypothesis of a profound convergence between these two schools of thought[54].

Rathenau's analysis was developed starting with the acknowledgement of the crisis experienced in Germany by the existing order.

This order had been profoundly influenced by Germany's attempt to recover its delay compared to Great Britain.

Great Britain had been the first to experience an industrial revolution and this allowed the country to assume a position of leadership at a global level and extremely strong contractual power as far as the economies of the rest of the world were concerned. This privileged position supported the creation of a planetary empire and allowed Great Britain to finance the development of a series of countries, the United States *in primis.* It made it possible for British companies to show extremely high profits which in turn allowed then to self-finance their development. It created the basis for the development of liberalism, which resulted in the beginning of a new phase in social development. In the British experience, entrepreneurs were the main players in this revolution, and asserted the role of a new managerial class, the bourgeoisie. Profit assumed the value of an objective of general interest.

54 Weber, M., *Il metodo delle scienze storico-sociali*, ed. it. Einaudi, Turin, 1958.

Having started its first industrial revolution later than Great Britain, Germany had been obliged to develop a different model, founded on far greater levels of centralisation than the British precedent.

The success achieved by Germany in closing the historical gap was at the time seen by Rathenau as the end of a cycle, thereby creating the possibility of "a new economy."

As a latecomer, Germany had to face a relative shortage of capital. On one hand the delay in the industrialisation of the German economic system, compared to the British, had obliged the economy to a more intense accumulation effort. This resulted in a rise in demand for capital. On the other hand, capital supply could not be self-financed to a sufficient extent. Having to face competition from consolidated British companies, German businesses and companies could not expect to achieve the same high levels of profit made by British companies in previous years[55].

In order to make up for this delay, the German economy had to activate new sources for financing investments. The most innovative aspect of the German model was the new circuit activated to fill this deficit, which consisted in the creation of the universal bank[56]. Thus the banking system assumed responsibility for ensuring that companies received short, medium and long-term capital and financing with a direct involvement in the accumulation process, in allocating resources and managing the companies financed[57].

The first German industrial revolution replicated the liberalism model, but differed from the traditional British model in some important aspects. There was not, as happened in the British experience, the entrepreneur at the centre of the market, acting in the general interest

---

55 Sommariva, A., Tullio, G., *German Macroeconomic History, 1880-1979*, McMillan, London, 1986.

56 Fontana, G., *Le vie dell'industrializzazione europea: sistemi a confronto*, Il Mulino, Bologna, 1997.

57 Teichova, A., Gourvish, A., Pogany, A. (eds), *Universal Banking in the 20th Century*, Elgar, Aldershot, 1994.

by maximising his profits. In the German model, the universal bank, with its own programming power, took centre stage, assuming responsibility for allocating resources so as to protect the general interest. The universal bank was influenced in its decisions by state authorities with greater intensity and in different ways compared to the influence exercised on entrepreneurs by British state authorities.

This model determined relative centralisation and the creation of an élite capable of controlling the economy, occupying strategic positions between the industrial and the banking sector. This élite in turn established relations with state power, thereby further increasing the level of centralisation in the broadest sense of the word. Rathenau acknowledged the contribution provided by this order to the country's modernisation with the development of the first industrial revolution, but he recognised these characteristics of the order implemented at the time as an obstacle to the implementation of a new more advanced order that appeared possible.

As an alternative to the existing order, Rathenau perceived the first signs of a new order, an economy based on a new relationship between the public and private sectors. This new economy was not an enlightened objective elaborated on by Rathenau with a normative approach. He perceived an unexpressed potential maturing within society that could only be understood from the perspective of a new interpretative paradigm. Rathenau envisaged a model of economy and society towards which Germany was evolving, one in which opposing powers did not obstruct progress. His approach was characterised more by interpretation than by establishing rules. Rathenau was the first to sense that Germany had embarked upon a model that today we call social market economy and one he generically called "a new economy".

The German economist perceived society's budding aspiration to participate in an organised manner in the decisions on which the system's future depended. The mix of public and private interests was counterbalanced by an increasingly strong desire to establish a new relationship between the public and the private, based on the acknowledgement of which functions should be assigned to the state, and the freedom to take initiatives on which the success of market liberalism depends.

Rathenau lived in an Atlantic cultural and economic environment. His company AEG and American-owned General Electric had entered an agreement to reduce competition on the global market. He was part of a small number of entrepreneurs who, already at the beginning of the century, had a global vision of the world economy and was therefore aware of what President Theodore Roosevelt had achieved in order to establish a new public-private order, opposing monopolies and remedying the market's failure to address unbalanced concentrations of capital. There were profound similarities with the American experience and the projects debated by German progressive liberals at the beginning of the century.

The need to reform public-private relations emerged clearly at the beginning of the 20th Century on both sides of the Atlantic. As previously mentioned, the more incisive measures were first adopted in the United States at the beginning of the century by President Theodore Roosevelt (1858-1919), who drafted the first coherent and effective anti-trust laws. His initiative was to be developed by his distant cousin Franklin D. Roosevelt (1882-1945), who in the Thirties launched the great reforms of the New Deal.

In the years between the Theodore and the Franklin D. Roosevelt presidencies, in Europe Rathenau elaborated theories and sponsored initiatives with very close links to the American experience. Rathenau's legacy was resumed after the war at the end of the Nazi tragedy and more clearly assumed the form of a social market economy[58].

58 Since the end of the Thirties social market economy became specific at a theoretical level; it became fully implemented in the years of German re-foundation.

This time-lag was not without consequences and had in the past been an obstacle to the development of synergies between neo-liberal experiences in the United States and in Europe. Today the passing of time seems to have diminished the importance of this initial time lapse. The growing convergence towards an increasingly integrated Atlantic area, and one that shares analogous problems, is a phenomenon becoming more and more clearly outlined and one with roots in events that developed at the beginning of last century.

A reference to the more specifically cultural aspects can contribute to a better understanding of these phenomena.

Rathenau was a member of the group of intellectuals who renewed German culture. Starting in 1907, Peter Behrens established a profound personal relationship with the Rathenau family. It was in his study that Gropius, Mies Van der Rohe and Le Corbusier formed their ideas[59]. This became an incubator for ideas that were to lead to the founding of the Bauhaus, the most innovative cultural adventure at a global level that would renovate architecture, design, art and music. In the industrial sector, Bauhaus forestalled the model of the clusters that achieved success at the beginning of the 21st Century within the context of a society of knowledge. Relations with Musil were dialectical and he included Rathenau as one of the characters in his novel entitled "The Man without Qualities"[60].

It was in this avant-garde cultural atmosphere that Rathenau's ideas took shape. His interlocutors interpreted all the emerging novelties, thereby anticipating the development towards which society was moving and this fuelled his thoughts and his initiatives[61].

See: Felice, F., *L'economia sociale di mercato*, Rubbettino, Soveria Mannelli, 2008.

59 Benevolo, L., *Storia dell'architettura moderna*, Laterza, Bari, 1960.

60 Musil, R., *L'uomo senza qualità*, ed. it. Einaudi, Turin, 1962.

61 One of the Pavia school's great historians, C.M. Cipolla, liked to repeat that in order to understand the past it is necessary to study the most important history

The same applied to the family of Presidents Theodore Roosevelt and Franklin D. Roosevelt. This family too was a reference point for a series of intellectuals who contributed to the modernisation of the United States. Jurists, economists, sociologists and members of America's cultural and scientific élite fuelled the reflections of these two presidents, committed to seize the epoch-making transformation the country was embarking upon.

In the United States the 20th Century brought a transformation of values, a crisis of the existing order and the birth of a new society. Traditional liberalism was replaced by Fordism and the managerial revolution[62].

Over a short period of time, in Germany economic development modified the social order previously founded on a landed aristocracy. Corresponding phenomena developed throughout the countries in continental Europe, albeit at different times and in different ways.

There is one difference clearly dating back to the historical period between the two world wars that must be underlined. A number of representatives of Rathenau's cultural world emigrated to the United States and some of the men of letters who influenced the ideas of President Franklin D. Roosevelt were Europeans. The cultural interdependence between the United States and Europe was at the time mainly moving in one direction, from Europe to the United States[63], thanks to the American democracy's capacity to develop a power of

---

books, while to understand the future one must visit art galleries. As far as the author knows, Cipolla did not include this statement in any of his books.

62 Schlesinger, A.M., *The coming of the New Deal*, Houghton Mifflin, Boston, 1959.

63 Rathenau died assassinated by a number of Nazi officers in 1922 while he was the Weimar government's Foreign Minister. A few years later, a similar albeit not quite so dramatic fate attended the members of the Bauhaus. The organisation was disbanded and its members sought refuge abroad, *in primis* Gropius in the United States. An original interpretation of the cultural atmosphere experienced by F.D. Roosevelt was provided by one of his most important advisors; see Monnet, J., *Mémoires*, op. cit.

attraction that anticipated the United States' leadership that emerged during World War II.

2.4 Relations between the public and private sectors

In order to outline a new economy capable of overcoming the crisis of the order in Germany in those years, Rathenau was obliged to address the crucial issue of relations between the public and the private. As mentioned previously, the German model of development differed from the British model in the diverse configuration of public-private relations.

In the model provided by classical liberalism, which emerged within the framework of the British industrial revolution, relations between the state and the market created the manner in which a division of power was achievable, in order to establish an evolutionary balance. The concept of a division of power refers firstly to state power, thus executive power, judicial power and legislative power. The market is set in the context as a "fourth power" in which civil society can present its demands for renewal.

Rathenau grasped that the German model of development, based on the universal bank, changed the role that classical liberalism assigned to the market. In the German experience the market is only partly set within a framework of a division of power, but becomes the setting for growing cooperation between the different state and private powers.

This transformation can be identified *in nuce* at the beginning of the century also in the United States, where thanks to initiatives undertaken by President Theodore Roosevelt, state powers assumed a leading role within the markets in order to guarantee their good functioning. This change emerged with growing clarity with the New Deal thanks to initiatives implemented by President Franklin D. Roosevelt.

Rathenau acknowledges that in the German experience the market is a place of cooperation between the various powers already before the American change sponsored by Presidents Theodore and Franklin D. Roosevelt. He questioned whether this tradition could be renewed, changing the relationship between the various powers present in the market. This was a profound innovation while respecting a degree of continuity. In Rathenau's system the market remains a setting for co-operation between the different powers. What changes in his analysis is the form of this cooperation.

Rathenau replaced the conflicting capitalism/socialism duo with public/private, not as conflicting, but as elements of a new shared order.

Theodore and Franklin D. Roosevelt on one hand, and Rathenau on the other, opened a new chapter in the history of western economics, the importance of which has not yet been fully appreciated a century later.

This new idea of public-private relations was to become increasingly important in the decades that followed, initially with the second industrial revolution and more lately with the current rise of a society of knowledge.

In order to define the potential of a development model based on new forms of public/private cooperation, to use Rathenau's words, a new economy, the German philosopher posed himself the problem of how one could guarantee the change from a centralised order to one open to new powers. Rathenau found the solution to this problem in the success of an order founded on what today would be described as subsidiarity, a word not yet created at the time.

To renew the German model, Rathenau addressed the complexity and the organisation of decision-making processes. The formation of an élite capable of controlling the political-economic system allowed Germany to experience its first industrial revolution and to embark upon a profound modernisation process. Rathenau identified the limitations of this order in centralisation, which leads to bureaucratisation and statism, obstructing the development of new powers in the market.

To establish a new order, Rathenau addressed an issue destined to become crucial for the success of a social market economy, consisting of how to reconcile the system's unity with the need to guarantee open forms of participation and the development of organised decision-making processes. This problem was not present in the experience developed in the United States at the beginning of the century because the country already had a strongly decentralised federal structure. The New Deal would have to address a diametrically opposite issue of how to guarantee an adequate level of centralisation without questioning the federal characteristics of the American constitutional order.

The relationship between the public and the private that had developed in Germany during the 19th century left as a legacy for the new century the centralistic order in which cooperation between powers had become gradually sclerotic. The new order Rathenau started to envisage was addressed at modifying this distorted intertwining of interests in order to return cooperation between powers to having characteristics open to innovation. The new order envisaged by Rathenau identified the objective to be achieved, not yet the changes, as being of a constitutional nature and one capable of becoming a permanent solution, as well as institutionalising the achievement of this objective. Rathenau has the historical merit of having founded the social market economy. A precise definition of this new order only began after a few decades, when the Nazi experience had brought the contradictions of the German model (centralised nationalism in more general terms) to its extreme consequences.

Rathenau analysed the complexity and organisation of decision-making processes paying specific attention to public-private relations, asking himself how one could establish an open order between players from different institutional levels, both in the vertical and horizontal sense, among players competing to carry out homogeneous or closely-linked functions.

Contemporary scholars commonly refer to the concept of subsidiarity in order to identify this transformation. This ideal *typus* had not yet been defined in the years during which Rathenau worked. It is possible that other interpretations may be put forth in the future to better seize and understand in greater depth, our knowledge of the evolution of the phenomena analysed here.

The market took shape in various ways over time and the same applies to statehood. These changes have accelerated in more recent times, first of all in more developed countries. These dynamics have made state/market relations complicated to the extent that they, State and market, have both undergone change.

Rathenau experienced the birth of this transformation and it is natural that his analysis could only provide an initial assessment. His great merit was having established a relationship between two phenomena, the importance of which only emerged in the decades that followed; a social market economy on one hand, and subsidiarity on the other. This intuition has provided an interpretation of great importance for better understanding the evolution of both phenomena and this dates back to their common origins[64]. An emblematic quotation from "A New Economy" states that:

> Die neue Wirtschaft wird (…) keine Staatswirtschaft sein, sondern eine der bürgerlichen Entschlußkraft anheimgestellte Privatwirtschaft, die freilich zum organischen Zusammenschluß, zur Überwindung innerer Reibung und zur Vervielfältigung ihrer Leistung und Tragkraft staatlicher Mitwirkung bedarf. Weder wird diese Mitwirkung abermals eine improvisierte sein, noch wird man sich mit beliebigem Angebot zufällig verfügbarer Kräfte begnügen, oder gar solcher, die ihren natürlichen Wirkungskreis noch nicht gefunden oder bereits verloren haben[65]

64 Rathenau, W., *L'economia nuova*, op. cit., page 62.

65 "The *new economy* (...) will not be a State economy, but a private economy ("market economy", as we might call it today, Editor's note) surveilled by civil (public)

Within this context, public-private relations result in intervention that orients powers towards the general interest while respecting their autonomy. Direct control, such as exercised by a state-owned company, can be a suitable means of compensating for the markets' deficiencies so as not to deny the role it plays. Referring specifically to business, Rahenau's vision introduced a border between state-owned companies and companies of a general interest[66]. These two types of enterprises have no ideological characteristics according to Rathenau, whose empiricism had its cultural roots in the British tradition.

In economics the very meaning of public intervention can assume different levels of importance in different periods and contexts. The long-term logic guiding intervention can be more important and influential than the intervention itself, although frequently its meaning is not correctly assessed if considered per se.

2.5 Social market economy and America's New Deal: two converging neo-liberal visions

The analysis of Rathenau's ideas presented, albeit briefly in previous pages, and bearing in mind the aspects not addressed in-depth, allows the emergence of a consonance with the American New Deal experi-

---

powers. It will be a private economy requiring collaboration from the State in order to achieve organic cohesion, to get over internal frictions and to multiply its performance and resistance. This collaboration shall not be improvised neither shall an arbitrary collection of forces be satisfactory, forces that might be by any chance available as they still haven't found – or they have lost - their natural allocation". Rathenau, W., *Die Neue Wirtschaft*, S. Fischer Verlag, Berlin, 1921, p. 75.

66 Companies of general interest was a concept established at a later date but that corresponds to a number of the elements contained in Rathenau's analysis. See Rossi, G. (edited by), *L'impresa europea di interesse generale*, Giuffrè, Milan, 2006.

ence. This point is of the utmost importance both for a correct historical reconstruction and perhaps even more so in order to assess possible future convergences at an Atlantic level.

The starting point from which Rathenau's ideas and work started differs from that of Franklin D. Roosevelt's reformist plans. The point of contact between these two experiences consists of the objective pursued within the diversity of the contexts[67].

The New Deal was developed within a greatly decentralised federal system. In order to develop federal policies a degree of centralisation was required. At the beginning of the century Germany was experiencing a period of great centralisation which tended to suffocate the innovating power of market liberalism.

In both cases a plan to renew liberalism emerged, in one case strengthening the federal state to remedy the failures of the market, and in the other changing consolidated order to implement a new economy.

Both Roosevelt and Rathenau envisaged an innovative balanced order between the public and private spheres in order to renew liberalism and project it towards the future.

The American and the European systems are often considered distant from one another due to the different values chosen over time. The consonance between Rathenau's anticipatory idea of a social market economy and the New Deal leads one to reassess the contact points rather than the diversities.

Those who underline the importance of the difference refer *in primis* to the individualism/solidarity alternative, in which the United States privileged individualism and continental Europe instead chose solidarity. This conflict is to a certain extent correct, all the more so when referring to the Calvinist tradition that characterizes part of

---

67 Kindleberger, A.P., *The World in Depression, 1929-1939*, Allenlane, London, 1973.

American society. It also appears distorted when referring to the increasing complexity of American society.

Every economic-social system is characterized by a confluence of different traditions, cultures, and communities bringing deeply-rooted values. It is an abstract to identify a dominant characteristic of a social-economic system, and all the more so when this system is an open and dynamic one.

With this awareness, a different value is assumed by the attempt to identify a number of characteristics of a system that can be used as the key for interpreting a number of constants identifiable within the order and the evolution of the system itself.

Identifying individualism as the dominant characteristic of the American social-economic system allows one to link a series of phenomena that have affected the development of society, the economy and statehood. Individualism in turn is motivated by a series of cultural, historical, religious and other causes. Stating that individualism is the dominant characteristic of the American model does not necessarily imply the disavowal of solidarity experiences that have certainly become rooted in the country, also in innovative ways.

Identifying solidarity as core Europe's social-economic system's dominant characteristic in turn allows for the systematization of a series of expertises and achievements typical of the Old Continent. In Europe, the different national traditions make it even more necessary than in the case of the Unites States to take into account the multiple declinations that the culture of solidarity can assume.

The use of the two *ideal typus* individualism-solidarity can contribute to a better understanding of some of the distances between the two Atlantic systems. The broad area placed between these two dominants creates the sphere within which experiences characterising both systems developed, a sphere in which it is easier to develop cooperation and forms of convergence. It is in referring to this same area that one can more easily see the rapprochement of these two systems, thereby overcoming the individualism-solidarity alternative.

It is important here to emphasize how assuming the point of view of an overcoming of the individualism-solidarity alternative is the perspective for correctly interpreting the positions assumed by W. Rathenau and Franklin D. Roosevelt.

Assuming this point of view is an interpretative and not a normative position. It involves understanding the harmony that developed between the New Deal and the social market economy since their very first manifestations. Both experiences arise as forms of neo-liberalism, for which they represented at the time the most advanced frontier.

This consonance has been underestimated for a long time due to the dyscrasia with which the two schools of thought developed. The New Deal's influence on the history of contemporary economics was to be far greater due to the implosion of the European system. One would have to wait for European economic-monetary union to see an autonomous European model, based on a social market economy once again present at an international level as an advanced frontier of development.

2.6. Social market economy. An evolving project

A social market economy as initially envisaged by W. Rathenau, is set within the framework of the secular liberalism tradition, which it tends to renovate albeit respecting its fundamental values[68].

At the end of the Thirties a theoretical debate reopened in Germany that is useful for enriching and better defining the very concept of social market economy[69], thanks to the contribution provided by various schools of thought and in particular by philosophers of both secular and Christian inspiration.

This marked the beginning of cross-fertilization between the Christian school of thought and liberalism's cultural traditions. This cross-fertilization would become full-blown after the war and would contribute to creating a climate of unity between German cultural-political elements supporting a shared commitment to rebuild the country.

It is not an objective of this book to reconstruct the debate that led to an increasingly clear outlining of a social market economy, *in primis* in Germany. It is instead our intention to seize a number of contributions that were the most influential in orienting the process that resulted in the definition of a social market economy and that can, in current conditions, be assessed on the basis of their more or less important relevance.

The first aspect one must emphasize is the continuity between Rathenau's work and ordoliberalism's perspective, which in 1936

68 Rathenau, W., *La triple dévolution*, Paris, 1921. The book is quoted and discussed by Villari, L., "Introduzione", in Rathenau, W., *L'economia nuova*, ed. it., op. cit.

69 An anthology of the work of philosophers who duelled the debate on social market economy has been curated with particular ability in seizing the most important aspects by Forte, F., Felice, F. (edited by), *Il liberalismo delle regole*, op. cit.

opened a new phase in the development of the very idea of a social market economy[70].

The prospect stated by ordoliberals, the liberalism of rules which is now the universally accepted definition, is founded on the idea that the economy is an element of society, and that posing the problem of a new order in the economy implies the need to pose the problem of a new order at a social and a political level[71].

Economic order should be perceived as an element of social-political order and all these elements should be taken to a constitutional level. Economists are called upon to address the interaction between the economic, material and formal constitution of the system within which it is set. The same applies, *mutatis mutandis*, for all scholars of other social disciplines.

This approach can be considered a development of the ideas expressed, still in an embryonic form, by Rathenau[72]. At the centre of the reflection there is a general political plan addressed at renewing existing order in an evolutionary manner. The reference to rules assumes a fundamental value in this plan. The area in which rules are established is the constitution, and rules are called upon to guarantee the implementation of the fundamental values that have the citizens' consensus.

This orientation leads to addressing the subject of statehood, and, more specifically, relations between the state and the market. From

70 Boehm, F., Eucken, W., Grossmann-Doerth, H., *Ordnung der Wirtschaft*, Kohlhammer, Stuttgart, 1936.

71 Ordoliberalism's approach underlines the interdisciplinary approach between the politological, economics, sociology, law and the other disciplines that allow one to understand the historical development. See Hasse, R.H., Schneider, H., Weigelt, K. (eds), *Social Market Economy. History, Principles and Implementation*, Schoening, Paderborn, 2008.

72 In the texts founding ordoliberalism's approach, the conceptual relationship with W. Rathenau's work is not valorised. It is legitimate to wonder whether this can at least to a certain extent be blamed on Rathenau's anti-Nazi stand, confirmed by his tragic death. One should remember that the manifesto of ordoliberalism was published in 1936 thereby proving the intellectual courage of its authors.

this perspective too one instantly observes the anticipatory importance of the analysis undertaken by W. Rathenau.

W. Eucken, and after him the tradition of the Freiburg School within the framework of Ordoliberalism, concentrated in particular on an aspect considered of decisive importance. They believed in a renewed relationship between the state and the market that went beyond liberalism's traditional order as well as the German centralist model. The new relationship outlined was aimed at establishing an order in which the market preserved the significance of a place of freedom and in which the state was called upon to protect such freedom, intervening when faced with the market's failure but not replacing it[73].

Ultimately, similarities with the New-Deal's neo-liberalism, mentioned in the analysis of W. Rathenau's work, became increasingly evident in contributions provided by W. Eucken and other economists from the Freiburg School. The German experience was sufficient to warn Eucken of the risks involved in statism, and he perceived how the state should be called upon to assume a renewed and more pervasive role in order to protect the balanced development of the market[74].

This approach was extended to social policies. It is not seen as an alternative to the market but as a condition for its balanced working. On this specific point, there was a profound assonance with Roosevelt's New Deal; agreement, at a more specifically theoretical level, with Luigi Einaudi's neo-liberalism is perhaps even clearer and more direct[75]. One firm point in Einaudi's ideas, often repeated in his publications, was the persuasion that social justice in an order founded on liberalism should be firstly based on an equal starting point for all citizens, and therefore access without privileges to the market.

73 Eucken, W., *I fondamenti dell'economia politica*, ed. it. Sansoni, Florence, 1951.

74 Goldschmidt, N., Wohlgemut, M., *Grundtexte zur friburger tradition der ordnung oekonomik*, Mohr, Tubingen, 2008.

75 Einaudi, L., *Prediche inutili*, Einaudi, Torino, 1954; see also Gigliobianco, A. (edited by), *Luigi Einaudi: libertà, economia e coesione sociale*, Laterza, Bari, 2010.

Free competition cannot be guaranteed by laissez-faire policies; it is a precious asset that must be protected by laws and by the state's regulating intervention. Once again the problem for Eucken and his group of thinkers was to avoid that this need for state regulation to protect the general interest should degenerate into forms of statism and bureaucratic centralism of any kind.

A role of particular importance in the assertion of a social market economy in the post-war period is universally acknowledged to Alfred Müller-Armack. He is attributed paternity of the phrase "social market economy"[76]. This author provided a dual contribution. On one hand he contributed to establishing a link between liberalism and the Christian culture, which was to orient the later development of a social market economy, while on the other hand he actively worked within the country's government contributing to the implementation of a social market economy as a strategic project for Germany's development and modernization[77]. His work later influenced the European Union as a whole towards a social market economy thereby activating a more long-term process[78].

Müller-Armack sensed how the synergy between political liberalism and Christian humanism could become the basis on which an order capable of merging freedom and solidarity could be created. It would be up to liberalism to renew the very meaning of freedom in Germany after the war, historicizing this value. It would in turn be Christian humanism that would simultaneously restore the meaning of solidarity. What was most important according to Müller-Armack, was

---

76 Grosser, D., Lange, Th., Müller-Armack, A., Neuss, B., *Soziale marktwirtschaft-gescichte-konzept-leistung"*, Kohlhammer, Stuttgart, 1988.

77 Müller-Armack, A., *Religion und wirtschaft geistes geschtiliche hinter guende unserer europaischen lebensform*, Kohlhammer, Stuttgart, 1959.

78 A. Müller-Armack was Chancellor Erhard's Foreign Minister when the Treaty of Rome that founded the EEC was signed. He contributed in particular to defining the rules of this treaty, which have remained the firm reference point for later development of European integration.

that these two great philosophical traditions should find themselves able to operate with a profound unity of intentions, with an overlapping of roles that corresponded to the synergy of their respective contributions. According to the authors of this book, with an interpretation not fully confirmed by Müller-Armack's publications, the German philosopher outlines a convergence between economic policies and social policies, overcoming the conflict present in both these policies, albeit at different levels of intensity and in different ways, in both these traditions. Müller-Armack's capacity to present social market economy as a cohesive and united model and not as the result of contingent convergences and thus destined to have a high level of flexibility over time between different traditions and values, was to have a political impact of the greatest importance. This qualifies a long-term project. Müller-Armack was fully aware that perceiving a social market economy as the programme for an alliance, however it may have been planned, of different political-cultural formations, would have reduced the project to a short-term economic instrument in which short-term realism would have surpassed the enlightened attempt to search for consensus in the creation of a model that would provide an alternative to capitalism, Stalinism and corporatism.

Thanks to Müller-Armack's contributions, the social market economy would be acknowledged as a model projected towards the 21st Century, capable of renovating Europe's great tradition of freedom and solidarity[79].

Müller-Armack clarified how a social market economy is not a mixed system reconciling freedom and solidarity with the government's appropriate role. In this system social progress is guaranteed by freedom which in turn is fuelled by social progress. It was this characteristic of German society that had to be acknowledged and exploited; the statement that their contribution of ideas was *in primis* in-

79 Peacock, A., Willgerondt, H. (eds), *German neo-liberals and the Social Market Economy*, Macmillan, London, 1989.

terpretative and only later would coherently become normative, applies to both Müller-Armack and Rathenau.

In this manner Müller-Armack led the German managerial class to reflect upon the Catholic Church's social doctrine that had until then influenced the country's culture to a relatively small extent. One decisive contribution in this sense was provided by Wilhelm Röpke, the most important representative of the Christian members of the group of social market economy's "Founding Fathers".

Röpke joins the debate on social market economy presenting an ethical motion. Moral order is essential in order to harmoniously allow the development of a juridical and economic order. Moral order, in particular, is the border separating liberalism from liberism[80], a market with no state from a market regulated by a state which must assume responsibility for guaranteeing that shared rules are respected.

Human activities take place within a cultural context, as acknowledged by all the scholars who forged the concept of a social market economy.

An unavoidable element that is of the utmost importance, when qualifying a cultural context, is moral order, according to Röpke's specific perspective. This interpretation characterizes all his work albeit declined in different forms in later publications[81].

Humankind achieves fulfilment living with a community, within institutions. This is one of the Church's traditional teachings that Röpke adopts to qualify social market economy as a form of new humanism. In this way, anticipating phenomena what would emerge only in the years that followed, Röpke presented a social market economy as an alternative to the crisis caused by post-modernity. He envisages a new humanism as an alternative to the lack of rules in a society characterised by institutions experiencing a crisis.

---

80 Croce, B., Einaudi, L., *Liberismo e liberalismo*, Ricciardi, Milan, 1957.

81 Röpke, W., *Civitas humana. I problemi fondamentali di una riforma sociale ed economica*, ed. it. Rizzoli, Milan, 1947.

In Röpke there is a spiritual vision that makes his contribution to the definition of a social market economy not entirely homogeneous compared to those of other aforementioned scholars. It is easier to discover profound points of contact between Röpke's ideas and work by the Italian Don Sturzo, rather than with some of the German philosophers who devoted their studies to a social market economy[82]. This communion of ideas with the work of Don Sturzo is a reminder of the importance of the Encyclicals that defined the Church's social doctrine as a source of inspiration for Röpke[83].

The attention Röpke paid to the Church's social doctrine contributed to his developing a growing awareness of the importance of a principle present in a social market economy, starting with Rathenau's work, consisting of a new statehood coherent with the new social-economic order. The new stateness is today described using the word "subsidiarity", which, as known, has become part of the politological lexicon as derived from the Church's social doctrine. This is a crucial aspect for fully understanding social market economy, as so far been historicized *in primis* in the German experience.

As already specified, the synthesis presented here does not aspire to be a reconstruction of the development of the concepts through which social market economy was experienced. The perspective adopted in our research reveals how social market economy is an evolving project. Having reached a fundamental cross-roads, where the possibility that social market economy may become a European project rather than one assumed only by core-Europe, acknowledging the historical development of the project assumes new importance. It

---

82 Felice, F., *Luigi Sturzo e l'economia sociale di mercato*, C.I.S.S., Rome, 2011; Guccione, E. (edited by), *Luigi Sturzo e la democrazia nella prospettiva del terzo millennio*, Olschki, Florence 2004; D'Addio, M. (edited by), *Opere scelte di Luigi Sturzo. Stato, Parlamento e Partiti*, Laterza, Bari, 1992; Palladino, G., *Don Sturzo oggi*, La Nuova Cultura Editrice, Naples, 1995.

83 Röpke, W., "Wirtschaftssystem und internationale ordnung", in AA.VV., *Scritti di sociologia e politica in onore di Luigi Sturzo*, Zanichelli, Bologna, 1954.

is necessary to understand what vision of a social market economy Europe will adopt and with which innovations compared to the past.

2.7 Freedom, solidarity, subsidiarity: the three fundamental principles of a social market economy

Any definition of social market economy inevitably results only in an approximation of its contents, as a direct consequence of the still on-going evolution of this order. If one refers to its qualifying contents, growing consensus has been achieved by the identification of the three fundamental principles on which social market economy is founded[84]. These principles are identified as freedom, solidarity and subsidiarity[85].

In previous pages attention has been devoted to the first two principles. Historically they were the first to become defined with greater clarity. Freedom and solidarity are fundamental values in the two main schools of thought which contributed to shaping the order founded on a social market economy in core-Europe's experience.

The principle of subsidiarity became defined in the European experience over recent decades. It was incorporated by social market economy in order to comply with the need, which emerged at the very beginning in Rathenau's work, to place new social-economic order within the framework of a new stateness.

The process through which new forms of stateness were formed was for a long time sensed rather than fully understood by scholars who most contributed to defining the order founded on social market

84 Nicholls, A.J., *Freedom with responsibility. Social market economy in Germany 1918-1963*, Clarendon Press, Oxford, 1994.

85 Quadrio Curzio, A., *Sussidiarietà e sviluppo. Paradigmi per l'Europa e per l'Italia*, Vita e Pensiero, Milano, 2003; Fenske, H., *Il pensiero politico contemporaneo*, ed. it. Il Mulino, Bologna, 2001.

economy[86]. Röpke's contribution is emblematic in this sense; he distinguishes between the "sick state" and the "healthy state" thereby emphasizing a not yet resolved intellectual requisite[87]. He criticizes the limitations of capitalism and collectivism, but when addressing the definition of new stateness implementing the principle of subsidiarity, his analysis does not go beyond the concept of decentralisation[88].

And yet, the Encyclical "Quadragesimo anno" dated 1931, had already provided a contribution to the definition of subsidiarity within the framework of the Church's social doctrine[89].

The principle of subsidiarity became clearer after the war thanks to a number of contributions; the most important were: a) the influence exercised by United Stated federalism on constitutional processes in Europe and *in primis* in Germany; b) the creation of a new European stateness that adopted subsidiarity as a fundamental constitutional principle; c) the development of the Church's social doctrine.

The third fundamental principal of social market economy, subsidiarity, did not experience an autonomous development within this school of thought; it was accepted because it answered an unresolved need and one clearly already identified by this school of thought.

This is an important aspect since it allows a better historicizing of the development of a social market economy in Europe and *in primis* in Germany; it was able to integrate in a process, providing its own

---

86 Galgano, F., *Le istituzioni dell'economia di transizione*, Zanichelli, Bologna, 1978.

87 Röpke, W., *Civitas humana*, op. cit.

88 On this subject Cotelessa believes that "in the perspective adopted by Röpke, the implementation of the principle of subsidiarity should be understood in the sense of a sort of *decentralism of default*". Cotellessa, S., "Introduzione", in Röpke, W., *Democrazia ed economia*, op. cit., p. 16.

89 It is legitimate to pose the problem of a relative intellectual delay shown by Röpke regards to the Church's social doctrine which was well-known to him.

contribution and in turn becoming enriched with contributions converging in this same process[90].

One must first consider American federalism's influence on constitutional processes in Germany and Europe. Immediately after the war the powers that won were posed the problem of guaranteeing Germany's future, while simultaneously preventing a third hegemonic attempt carrying the risk of a third World War. The difficulties experienced in reconciling these two objectives were at the basis of a widespread debate. Many projects were prepared, some filled with fears concerning Germany's capabilities, with others oriented at setting Germany within an international framework capable of guaranteeing balance and preventing a return to the past with constructive solutions.

History proves that the second tendencies prevailed on the basis of two fundamental projects. The first consisted in imposing on Germany a federal constitution based on the model provided by the American one. This project succeeded well beyond the expectations of the proposers themselves, since a federal organisation corresponded to the history of the country that for centuries had consisted of small autonomous states that in many cases coincide with today's Lande.

The second project of fundamental importance was the transfer of power from the national to the European level. In founding the ECSC, Monnet allowed Germany to recreate its heavy industry, no longer as the basis of power of a national government, but as a member of a European economic sector, governed by a supranational authority. The development of the integration process over the years that followed was to confirm the far-sightedness of Monnet's initiative.

It is important to bear in mind later developments as far as Germany's constitutional organisation is concerned. The federal constitution imposed by the Allies was replaced after a few years with an

---

90 Ferrari, F. (edited by), *Federalismo, sistema fiscale, autonomie. Modelli giuridici comparati*, Donzelli, Rome, 2010.

autonomously drafted federal constitution. This confirms the success of the project that was able to develop democratically[91].

One instantly perceives how the success of social market economy in Germany should be linked to these two great projects with which a profound synergy emerges. Both the federal constitution and the European unification process following Monnet's model, strengthened the federal aspects of social market economy[92].

Over the long term, the greatest impact was exercised by the adoption of subsidiarity as the constitutional principle that was the cornerstone of European integration. As seen in previous pages[93] the integration process developed, outlining a new stateness founded on subsidiarity. This development was not a foregone conclusion. Each stage of the integration process involved choices between alternative options[94]. In particular, two basic alternatives were always present every time a choice of constitutional importance was made. A first alternative was the option involving a more centralised federal model, ultimately copying the American experience[95]. A second alternative was the option involving a federal model with a lower level of centralisation, sufficient for guaranteeing efficiency while respecting the prerogatives of member states.

Faced with these two alternatives, it is legitimate to address the issue of which presented the solution with the strongest points. The subject can be equally addressed in terms of the wishes and the per-

91 Jozzo, A., Velo, D., "L'autonomia della Banca Centrale in Italia e in Europa", op. cit.

92 Erhard, L., *Benessere per tutti*, ed. it. Garzanti, Milano, 1957; Erhard, L., *La politica economia della Germania. Per un'economia sociale di mercato*, ed. it. Garzanti, Milan, 1962.

93 See Chapter I.

94 Albertini, M., *Tutti gli scritti*, Il Mulino, Bologna, various years.

95 Bognetti, G., *Lo spirito del costituzionalismo americano*, Giappichelli, Turin, 1998.

spective of the values that each player in this process brought to the table[96].

In order to assess whether or not such reasons will remain in the future, and to what extent, for our analysis, it is more important to understand the reasons for which the less centralised form of statehood, and one more oriented towards subsidiarity, prevailed[97].

One fundamental reason should be searched for in the restricted development of foreign policy and defence for Europe as a whole and for the member states individually considered. International commitments, both at a social-economic level and in the defence sector, are a centralizing element found in the historical experiences of most states[98]. The integration process developed within a privileged international context. American leadership at a global level and Atlantic relations between the United States and Europe have allowed Europe to concentrate its energies on internal development, relying on the ability of its American ally to guarantee peace and stability on the Old Continent. This order has lasted since the end of the war until today and it is only recently that the possibility of a revision of the European Union's international role has emerged.

Thus Europe was able to become a workshop in which a new forms of statehood founded on subsidiarity took shape[99]. These statements apply to the European Union as a whole and apply even more to Germany which, as a direct consequence of hegemonic attempts twice in the 20th Century, has not developed an international political initiative that corresponds to the country's economic power. Civil society was able to create forms of participation and assumed responsibility in

---

96 Padoa-Schioppa, T., *Il governo dell'economia*, Il Mulino, Bologna, 1997.

97 Constantinesco, V., Pierré-Caps, G., *Droit constitutionnel*, Paris, PUF, 2004.

98 Robbins, L., *Il federalismo e l'ordine economico internazionale*, ed. it. Il Mulino, Bologna, 1985; Einaudi, L., *Le cause economiche della guerra*, Capolago, 1944.

99 Palermo, F., *La forma di stato dell'Unione Europea*, CEDAM, Padova, 2005.

ways that would have been impossible in the presence of a high degree of centralization[100].

European peace, in the broadest sense, has allowed social-economic and institutional development founded on subsidiarity.

A social market economy was therefore able to develop, starting with a core-Europe, acknowledging the potential offered by the expansion of subsidiarity.

In projecting this analysis towards the future, it is legitimate to wonder whether in current conditions, social market economy can extend its influence to the entire European Union, assuming the value of content qualified as Economic Union. It is also legitimate to ask whether, parallel to this enlargement of its influence, a social market economy could be elaborated on, *in primis* in the countries it which is has taken root, acknowledging and complying with the requests presented by a new humanism. The alternative is a centralizing process that would challenge the characteristics developed so far by the unification process and would marginalize the role played by social market economy.

2.8 Social market economy at the dawn of a new humanism

In order to predict social market economy's possible success and further development, this order can be set within the framework of the current debate between post-modernity on one hand and new humanism on the other. It is in the way possible to perceive a number of aspects that are certainly significant.

100 Weiler, J., Wind, M., *European Constitutionalism beyond the State*, CUP, Cambridge, 2003.

It is widely believed that post-modernity has entered a phase of decline, having fuelled and justified regressive phenomena, and that a new phase is beginning, starting with the more advanced systems, characterised by growing consensus for the values of a new humanism. The hypothesis adopted by the author is that social market economy is set within this second scenario, described here with the word new humanism[101], a collocation that increases the possibilities of social market economy becoming deeply rooted.

This collocation, with social market economy as an alternative to post-modernity and coherently with new humanism, obliges one to explain the identification of the contents adopted in this book[102].

In our interpretation, post-modernity is qualified by three fundamental ideas: an absolute relativism, a vision of the individual in a society with no rules, and a radical underestimation of the role played by institutions. These concepts are interrelated in a manner that results in them appearing to be aspects of a single idea.

Post-modernity theorizes the weakening of the great interpretative systems, of universal values, of ideologies. This threatens the very possibility of processing totalizing interpretative models and rules. This results in the creation of an immense void that can be filled by systematic doubts, pragmatism, and by the coexistence of different perspectives of the world without a search for criteria of truth. It is the kingdom of relativism, fragmentation and complexity acknowledged as the founding basis of the new world[103].

In this way post-modernity renounces faith in a path that makes sense, humankind's capacity to plan and implement a historical route to assert universal values in the world. In post-modernity, there is no

---

101 Habermas, J., *La crisi della razionalità nel capitalismo futuro*, ed. it. Laterza, Bari, 1975.

102 This book is not specifically addressed at analysing in depth this subject of both sociological and philosophical importance. See Vattimo, G., *La fine della modernità*, Garzanti, Milan, 1985.

103 Prigogine, I., *Le leggi del caos*, ed. it. Laterza, Bari, 1993.

place for transcendence; it is an extraneous body, even more so than universal values, to the extent that it cannot be reconciled with the relativism of post-modernity.

Post-modernity does not address the problem of whether one should bring order to chaos or interpret it; it does not search for interpretative criteria, which would inevitably result in orienting thought and action. It accepts chaos and exists without certainties, uninterested in the very concept of truth[104].

In presenting this schematization, we explained that it is our interpretation. This statement corresponds to the fact that in the post-modern school of thought it not possible to find a self-definition, a manifesto for this philosophy. The post-modern addresses itself and the world it exists in, in the same manner, and just as it rejects all ideologies it also tends not to self-define itself[105].

A full description of post-modernity can only be made by those placed outside this philosophy. Those set within the post-modern perspective participate personally in the indeterminateness that qualifies its perspective of the world.

Post-modern man, to the extent he renounces to embrace universal values and the great interpretative systems and to pursue projects capable of implementing a historical process, condemns himself to solitude and bewilderment. It is this second concept that in our opinion identifies post-modernity.

This concept results in a series of corollaries. In the absence of orientations founded on values, post-modern man is pressed towards hedonism and to a life with no rules. This creates a growing void for alternative behaviours that do not need to be founded on values; entertainment, communication and syncretism provide a stage on which it is possible to perform a play with no story.

---

104 Foster, H. (edited by), *Postmodern Culture*, The Cromwell Press, Trowbridge, 1983.

105 Lyotard, J.F., *La condizione post-moderna*, ed. it. Feltrinelli, Milan, 1982.

The absence of values and rules, on one hand, and on the other the negation of the role played by institutions are interdependent aspects justifying one another from a post-modern point of view. In this manner the individual finds himself acting, whether with greater or lesser awareness is irrelevant, in the void of a world perceived without values and that he increasingly causes to experience a crisis denying the role played by institutions.

There is broad consensus among those who have analysed these behaviours in describing post-modern man as an individual using increasingly less rationality, replacing it with emotions, feelings and extemporaneous opinions. Opinion polls become the main means for understanding the changing orientations of a humankind without a culture anchored to certainties.

Individuals embracing post-modernity are urged to live as actors who experience with radical disbelief a solitary existence, without feeling the need for dialogue and relations with others and the need to respect order guaranteed by institutions.

In the interpretation of post-modernity outlined here, the underestimation of institutions plays a central role. It identifies a rift with other schools of thought, the results of which may turn out to be of an importance that for the moment can only be imagined[106].

The underestimation of institutions is important for post-modernity also because it provides the connection between this school of thought, radical neo-liberism and globalisation. The interrelation between these three forces profoundly influenced the second half of the 20th Century. The reference to globalisation allows for historicizing and consequently a better understanding of both post-modernity's development and that of radical liberism.

The prospect of a new humanism and the valorisation of social market economy, as a positive reaction, arose from the crisis experi-

106 Spaemann, A., *Per la critica dell'utopia politica*, ed. it. Angeli, Milan, 1995.

enced by this vast movement, generally synthesized with the word 'globalization', and that also includes the theories of post-modernity and neo-liberism.

2.9 Globalization, post-modernity and radical liberism *versus* new humanism and a social market economy

One of the fundamental aspects that, as stated in previous pages, defines post-modernity, consists of the underestimation of institutions. This aspect should be set in relation to the globalization process and with the radical liberist economic theories that are its ideology[107].

In the second half of the 20th Century there was an acceleration of the internationalization process. This process was oriented by leading countries, *in primis* the United States, and by international institutions founded with the specific objective of supporting and providing order to the development of cooperation. This balance between the development of international markets and the authorities' capacity to develop adequate governance progressively experienced a crisis, to the extent that the market developed increasingly, while state authorities saw the effectiveness of their initiative diminish. It is not the specific intention of this book to analyze in-depth the reasons for this dualistic development; it sufficient here to refer to the phenomenon and understand its impact on the subject at the centre of our analysis.

The different dimensions of the now global market and states made the market increasingly *legibus solutus*. The weakness of international institutions prevented them from assuming the role of governors of the global market and also rendered limitedly effective their legislative role.

107 Velo, D., *La grande impresa federale europea. Per una teoria cosmopolitica dell'impresa*, Giuffrè, Milan, 2004.

This development is in contradiction with the model provided by liberalism which resulted in harmonious relations between the state and the market; it corresponds to the liberist model which has denied the role played by the state and affirmed the market's supremacy. This development created opportunities for those having greater contractual power who used the lack of regulations to their own advantage[108].

Radical liberism has theorised globalization as a totally positive event, coherently with its idea of the superiority of market mechanisms compared to the regulating role of public institutions. Liberism, all the more so in its more radical forms, saw in the global market, deprived of institutions of reference of a same geographical size, an opportunity for affirming its ideology and implementing a corresponding order[109].

According to the classical liberalist approach, the birth of a global market should have been accompanied by the development of an institutional order capable of governing the market in its new configuration. The precedent set by European unification proves that an evolutionary project of this size is realistic, on condition that new adequate forms of statehood are found[110]. In a projection towards the future, the hypothesis that innovative forms of statehood could become outlined at a global level is possible, as they have already formed gradually in Europe to govern a market that extended beyond national borders. Liberism has denied this possibil-

108 Zamagni, S. (a cura di), *Economia, democrazia, istituzioni in una società in trasformazione*, op. cit.

109 One must emphasize the profound difference between the aforementioned liberist approach and that of liberalism. Liberalism sees the market as a reality within a state order responsible for protecting the general interest rather than particular interest that develop based on the initiatives of individual operators. A market in the absence of a state is not part of the cultural heritage of liberalism's tradition. See Croce, B., Einaudi, L., *Liberismo e liberalismo*, op. cit.; Croce, B., *Etica e politica*, Laterza, Bari, 1945; Einaudi, L., *Il buongoverno*, Laterza, Bari, 1954.

110 Models of statehood referable to the classical federal organisation, to the principle of subsidiarity, to multi-level governance, and to polyarchy have been experimented in the course of the European integration process. On this issue see the analysis developed in Chapter I and the bibliographical references quoted.

ity establishing an order alternative to the one provided by liberalism's model.

The impact of liberism's success has been all the more important since it also profoundly influenced internal order at a national level. The liberist perception of the market's superiority over public institutions has spread to all levels. Having matters run by managers has been established as the criteria on the basis of which public authorities run affairs, thereby also re-orienting institutions to the market's supremacy, taking action on their *modus operandi*. Systems have become homogenized, adopting the globalization model and translating it into the guideline criteria for reorganizing the current order, each time depending on the institutions or the rules subjected to the homogenizing process. Liberism in this manner became the dominant economic ideology in the last part of the 20th Century.

The homogeneity that profoundly links liberism and post-modernity is totally evident. Post-modernity can be understood as a philosophical perspective within which radical liberism is set, as the economic aspect of this school of thought. The interrelation of these points of view has provided a historical-philosophical justification for globalisation, in the forms it has assumed, becoming historicised in the last decades of the century[111].

Globalisation, radical liberism and post-modernity have merged, assuming the role of a general model for society and the economy.

A social market economy can be perceived as an alternative order. In order for it to be considered an alternative order it requires greater status, on one hand in its philosophical aspects and on the other in its political-economic ones, therefore in its capability to offer a renewed model for governing the economy and society.

Neo-humanism can be considered as the front-line as far as the values of social market economy are concerned. This is an hypothesis founded on an ongoing reflection that has begun but not yet matured, fuelled by contributions from both liberalism and the Christian world.

---

111 Beck, U., Giddens, A., Lash, S., *Modernizzazione riflessiva*, ed. it. Asterios, Trieste, 1999.

Humankind's overall development requires an institutional order within which freedom and solidarity are able to develop. A new humanism can become historicized within an inescapable relationship between each single individual and his community of reference, in an institutional framework capable of guaranteeing confidence in relationships[112].

The reference to the development of institutions for the Community sets relations between new humanism and a social market economy in a specific historical framework. Subsidiarity and federalism are the principles that in Europe inspired the unification process's forms of government. They are the reference point for those who place themselves in a perspective of governing the global market and to create institutions capable of guiding the convergence of states towards the progressive creation of a global democratic order.

Subsidiarity is a founding principle of social market economy. It is the cornerstone constitutional principle of the European Union and the principle that make unification processes possible, while respecting diversity, in other regional federations and between regional federations.

The process thereby outlined is a path of progress that can be provided with meaning only by a *telos*. Order founded on new humanism, a social market economy, subsidiarity and federalism, in our opinion, aspires to assume the value of an objective[113].

The meaning of interaction between a social market economy, new humanism and subsidiarity has not been adequately studied in depth[114].

The integration of economies at an international level is an inescapable historical process. This process involving increasing internationalisa-

112 See also the broadminded reflections in a research then devoted to specialist issues; Benedetti, A., *Certezza pubblica e "certezze" private*, Giuffrè, Milan, 2011.

113 Lombardi Vallauri, L., *Corso di filosofia del diritto*, Milani, Padova, 1981; Baumann, Z., *Voglia di comunità*, ed. it. Laterza, Bari, 2011.

114 Felisini, D., Velo, D., "L'Unione Europea e la società europea", in AA.VV., *L'Unione Europea e la società europea*, Jean Monnet Interregional Centre of Excellence, Pavia, 2010.

tion can be experienced following different reference models. Globalisation, liberism and post-modernity outline an internationalisation process – and within it social development - governed by market forces. The European experience proves how an internationalisation process can be governed by institutions, until a more advanced statehood is set up, based on a social market economy, subsidiarity and new humanism. If this development process continues, Europe will increasingly be able to strive to play the role of a workshop in which an order capable of establishing itself at a global level could be defined.

Interaction between federal integration, a social marker economy, subsidiarity and new humanism is at the centre of a debate that culture is fuelling with difficulty[115].

The novelty we are experiencing is the centrality of humankind. The possessive individualism asserted by post-modernity states the centrality of the market and not of humankind. Subsidiarity, social market economy and new humanism set humankind at the centre of the institutions, as well as in relations between institutions. Globalisation and liberism place at the centre of attention the mechanisms regulating the market perceived more important that the people in it. Social market economy and new humanism see humankind as the leading player of a development that makes sense, that historicizes the values of freedom and solidarity.

---

115 North, D.C., *Istituzioni, cambiamento istituzionale e evoluzione dell'economia*, ed. it. Il Mulino, Bologna, 1994; Habermas, J., *La costellazione postnazionale. Mercato globale, nazioni e democrazia*, ed. it Feltrinelli, Milano, 2002; Papisca, A., "Europe 2020: what Compass, what Soul, which kind of Architecture for the EU Governance? The Need of Human Rights Mainstreaming", in *Peace Human Rights*, 3/10.

Chapter III. Economic Union and the Problem of Rules

3.1 Economic union and the European Union's fundamental constitutional principles

The establishment of economic union poses two problems. Firstly it imposes the need to define the composition of this union. On the basis of the analysis developed in Chapter II, the crucial objective consists in defining which model of social market economy is capable of achieving the necessary consensus.

Secondly, establishing economic union implies the ways in which powers will necessarily be transferred from a national to a European level, and thus which institutions and rules will guarantee the implementation of economic union.

These two problems are interdependent. Instating a shared model of a European social market economy poses the problem of whether a minimum level of implementation should be defined that must be respected by all member states. A similar problem arose in translating fundamental rights, already fully integrated in the Lisbon Treaty, into provisions to be immediately applied. The precedent set by the United States is exemplary. The New Deal introduced federal measures to declare the principle of solidarity, overcoming the legislation of individual states that did not guarantee all citizens with a minimum level of welfare. This process, started during the Thirties, is still ongoing.

A constitutional conflict could result in a conflict between on the one hand the principle of subsidiarity, and on the other, decisions aimed at homogenizing, within limits, the social-economic systems of member countries.

The size of the European budget, *rebus sic stantibus*, is insufficient for allowing European institutions to assume significant direct financial responsibility[116].

As far as the second order of problems is concerned, the creation of a European governance of the European economy poses a number of more important alternatives and it is on these that this analysis will concentrate.

As happened for monetary union, economic union is destined to become a new phase in the European constituent process. The problems of constitutional importance that will have to be addressed are, *in primis*:

- which competences should be transferred to the European level;
- which European institutions will be able to perform these tasks;
- which charters will be responsible for guaranteeing the correct use of these competences.

Once again, the difficulties experienced in finding solutions to these problems arise from the fact that Europe does not have a written constitution to guide the unification process, but has already embarked upon a constituent process in "stages" running parallel to the expansion of integration[117].

One solution in a first stage can be found in a change of the material constitution, and it is only feasible to envisage the consolidation of a new economic order in terms of a formal constitution in a second phase. In conceptual terms this presents the risk of confusing the management of the transition with the definition of long term objectives. These two aspects should be kept rigorously distinct since they are of

116 This point will be addressed in the coming pages when debating the optimal size of the community's budget.

117 The Lisbon Treaty is a first European constitution in the formal sense,. It is *in primis* characterized by having given order to the acquisitions of the past and stated clearly the principles and inspiring values of the unification process. Those looking for guidelines for implementing economic union will find in this Treaty confirmation of the broad range of choices available.

a different nature. This problem is a typical characteristic of the European unification process[118]. As previously mentioned, due to its fundamental characteristics, the implementation of European unity has required a radical change in the manner in which national change processes have traditionally been devised.

At a national level institutions are an anchor bolt, while implemented policies evolve. At a European level, the unification process has been obliged to change institutional order every time the need to develop new policies was addressed[119].

At a national level it is physiological for policies to be decided establishing a transition period and all the more so if they are long term ones, while at a European level the definition of the transition period precedes that of institutional solutions[120].

To clarify the importance of these remarks, a number of indications can be found in a first outline proposed at the end of paragraph 2.1, "From monetary union to economic union: continuity and discontinuity in the unification process."

At the time, the restrictions envisaged as having to be respected by economic union were considered negative and such restrictions can be understood as rules of conduct. From a positive perspective, they imply an economic union resulting in an alternate order[121].

---

118 For an in-depth analysis of this approach see, Velo, D., "Emergence de l'ECU face au dollar dans les relations monétaires internationales", in AA.VV., *Les rélations communautes européennes-Etas Unis*, Economica, Paris, 1987.

119 Albertini, M. (edited by Mosconi, N.), *All papers*, Vol. I – IX, op. cit.

120 This inversion can, at least to a certain extent, be blamed on the fact that at a European level all that is new must converge with the consolidated interests of member states. This results in transitions assuming the characteristics of phases during which consensus for the final objective pursues is obtained.

121 Montani, G., "The Government of the Economy in Europe. A post-Keynesian approach", in *The European Union Review*, 3/98.

Monetary union has affirmed the centrality of fiscal policy as a direct consequence of the neutralization of monetary policy sanctioned by the ECB's charter.

Economic union will strengthen the centrality of fiscal policies. Fiscal federalism provides a partial solution to this problem and is yet to be defined in order to ensure it corresponds to the characteristics of the integration process[122].

The definition of public and private areas goes beyond fiscal federalism's dimension and the same applies to relations between the state, the markets and society in more general terms.

These hypotheses outline a long term perspective and do not respond to contingent motivations. They are instead important for understanding the ongoing process and do not define dogmatic, non-negotiable objectives, nor are they based on concerns regarding the management of the transition.

A dividing line between national and European responsibilities needs to be explored, as does one between the responsibilities of society, the markets and the state at all levels. This is the most important constitutional aspect in the project for economic union as it has begun to become outlined, albeit still in a confused manner[123].

---

122 Emerson, E., *La nuova economia europea*, ed. it. Il Mulino, Bologna, 1990; Pernice, L., "Multilevel constitutionalism and the Treaty of Amsterdam: European Constitution making revisited", *Common Market Law Review*, 36/99.

123 A simplified perspective, oriented at transitions and contingencies, results in the identification of two opposing areas. On the basis of this interpretation it is up to individual countries to rebalance the imbalances inherited in order to progress towards the new order of Economic Union. It is up to European institutions to guarantee development and innovation, activating new means for supporting investments. This division must be historicized; per se it has no value, even as a first approximation for a programmes to orient one's thoughts on the fundamental characteristics of economic union.

3.2 Economic union and the problems posed by regulations

Monetary union is a precedent for assessing the importance of defining rules to be respected, both as a condition for progressing towards the creation of economic union and, more in general, to make progress in the integration process[124]. Monetary unification, as analyzed in previous pages, achieved completion only following the clarification and definition of the qualifying contents of the ECB charter and, with them, the creation of rules to be respected in governing monetary union.

The same must apply to economic union, just as, within this context, it applies to fiscal federalism. It is not only a question of defining the distribution of functions and resources between the European Union's various institutional levels, but also rules for managing these competences and the resources available. As a necessary corollary, this implies the definition of guarantees to ensure such order is respected.

A coherent management of public finance by the E.U.'s institutions, based on common rules, is necessary for a number of reasons which are ultimately based on the fact that the financial behaviour of each institution has repercussions on all other institutions, and, all the more so, depending on the extent of the deviance and importance of the institution involved. This applies to all unions and is a more binding issue within a union based on the principle of subsidiarity, the European Union *in primis*.

The principle of subsidiarity protects the autonomy of each institution. This autonomy experiences a crisis when some institutions have the power to arbitrarily modify the distribution of resources to

124 Tsoukalis, L. (edited by), *The Political Economy of International Money*, Royal Institute of International Affairs, London, 1985.

their own advantage, increasing the resources available by resorting to imposition and debt[125].

The principle of subsidiarity has oriented fundamental constitutional choices made in the course of the integration process. It is called upon to orient the fundamental choices that will be made to define economic union in order to guarantee its coherence with the process within which it will be set. Should economic union be achieved on the basis of a centralizing process, this would require a radical change in the very principles on which the integration process is founded. A re-orientation of the integration process towards levels of greater centralization is an hypothesis, but only on condition there is adequate consensus and a full awareness of the implications posed by such an option. In the absence of these conditions, one can predict the emergence of negotiations that would lead to a crisis of the integration process itself[126]. A centralization process is more easily envisaged in the presence of international tension endangering the European Union's security.

These considerations apply to the economic order that will be established between the European level and member states. They also apply, *mutatis mutandis*, to relations between the various institutional levels that exist within member states. In the context of an order founded on subsidiarity, this also applies to relations between institutions placed at the same level in a horizontal sense[127].

---

125 When a number of institutions control the Central Bank, they can obtain an arbitrary modification of the distribution of resources in their own favour, resorting to the creation of a monetary basis. The ECB charter has tended to neutralize this possibility affirming its own autonomy.

126 For a more in-depth analysis see: Velo, D., "The European Social Market Economy in the Economic and Monetary Union", *Peace Human Rights*, about to be published.

127 Müller-Graff, P.C., "Subsidiarity as a legal principle", *The European Union Review*, 1/96.

These schematic remarks are also valid for understanding the impact on social order. A social market economy is a model for social-economic and institutional order coherent with economic union, on condition it is perceived in terms of subsidiarity.

This perspective allows one to understand the levels of freedom with which European society will be able to reorganize itself during the coming decades. In order for this process to be implemented in an orderly manner, the role played by rules will be fundamental.

It is the author's opinion that the fundamental rules debated can be summarised in three principles; zero inflation, zero deficit, zero debt. The first rule was introduced during the integration process by monetary union. The second and third rules were mentioned but not adequately specified by the Maastricht Treaty. They are predictably the fundamental prerequisite on which economic union and a European social market economy's development will depend[128].

3.3 The size of the budget

The rejection of monetary sovereignty by states that joined the monetary union has increased their desire to maintain control over fiscal policies, as well as the possibility of resorting to sovereign debt, the only means now available for governing internal economic events with a degree of significant, albeit decreasing autonomy.

This position has postponed to a later date the development of fiscal federalism, thereby extending the transition period[129].

---

128 Social market economy demands addressing the subject of rules far more directly compared to economic union. What is more relevant is the importance of rules both for economic union and for a social market economy.

129 This orientation is fuelled in some countries by the fear that there may be internal evolution less successful than in other member countries. The same applies

Countries that are part of monetary union have heterogeneous characteristics regarding many aspects of the economy, while their resources differ as do the characteristics of their productive sectors and laws having a more direct economic impact. In order to address the consequences of these diversities, in the absence of an efficient European governance of the European economy, one understands the desire of national governments to maintain a number of means of intervention having greater impact. This desire is ultimately justified by fear that a conflict between European general interests and the specific interests of an individual state may arise without the means for this conflict to be mediated by European institutions[130]. Such prudence also derives from an awareness, in countries with a less efficient administration, of predictable delays in developing a national fiscal policy capable of playing the role European monetary union assigns to it.

The certainties of the past assume particular importance when compared to change processes that are partly not yet defined.

Unification processes do not always guarantee the homogenization of the entire area involved. Differences dating back to starting points can last over time, even if unification succeeds in guaranteeing high levels of development. This also applies to the various areas that create each member state. Regional policies have a European and a national dimension. It is necessary to historicize the advantages that can be provided on one hand by a new order at a European level, and on the other by maintaining previously experimented solutions. An ab-

---

to the possibility that there may be asymmetrical shocks. Economic theory has not yet assessed sufficiently analytically to what extent these concerns are typical of a transition phase and to what extent they derive from phenomena of a structural kind. See Praussello, F., "Flaws in the Design of EMU: the Role of Asymmetric Shocks of Federal and National Origin", *The European Union Review*, 3/10.

130 Majocchi, A., *Il coordinamento delle politiche nel nuovo modello di federalismo fiscale*, Pavia University, Pavia, 2004.

stract option favouring these alternatives may degenerate into an ideological perspective not attentive to verification processes[131].

These uncertainties have resulted in a postponement of the drafting of an optimal European budget for ensuring the functionality of economic and monetary union. *Per se* these problems suggest that the objective of a definition of a complete model for fiscal federalism may be achieved after quite a long transition period, during which partial progress could be made. Consequently, the optimal size of the European budget will remain an unresolved issue for some time to come. In truth, the very nature of the problem has not yet been adequately addressed.

The debate that has developed for some time concerning the size of the E.U.'s budget can be outlined in number of consolidated positions in favour of a larger budget with a number of positions expressing doubts[132].

Those who support the need to increase the European budget, refer at an empirical level to the American experience. At a theoretical level the basic argument put forth by those seeing a need to increase the E.U.'s budget, refer to the greater effectiveness of expenditure concentrated at a federal level in various areas of intervention. When addressing international relations, the argument developed in favour of increasing the budget is based on the fact that centralizing expenditure at a European level is a prerequisite in more than one area for allowing Europe to speak with one voice, thus providing its initiatives with greater effectiveness compared to individual national initiatives not linked to one another.

---

131 The redistribution of revenue can occur in different ways in different areas within a federal system organised on the basis of the principle of subsidiarity. The defence of their own areas of competence undertaken by states cannot be assessed ignoring the context within it is set. See Eichengreen, B., *The European Economy since 1945. Coordinated Capitalism and Beyond*, Princeton University Press, Princeton, 2007.

132 Emerson, E., *La nuova economia europea*, op. cit.

The European Commission's traditional position has always been in favour of increasing the budget, so as to provide a more effective contribution to shared macro-economic objectives and to implement economic policy capable of ensuring the European economic system's development and stability.

The fact that the community budget has not been significantly increased bears witness *per se* to the fact that the objective has not yet acquired adequate consensus. The arguments mentioned at the beginning of this paragraph indicate how the budget's optimal size remains an unresolved issue not yet defined through a sufficiently in-depth analysis. New theoretical positions have more recently radically questioned whether the optimal size of the community's budget really needs to be larger than the current one.

The first consideration among those agreeing with this new position refers to the role assumed by public authorities within most advanced systems. They are strengthening their directing, coordinating and programming capabilities in a variety of sectors, while reducing their role as the direct providers of services. In this sense the health sector is emblematic. In a constantly increasing number of countries, these services are entrusted to private operators, to authorities, with innovative forms of public-private cooperation.

New European statehood is set within this framework. It is legitimate to state that European institutions have privileged this evolution to a relatively greater extent than other institutional levels of the E.U.. This reduces the importance of the European Union's budget and thus increases the importance of other forms of financing to fund the operational capabilities of those delegated to provide services[133].

At a European level, the impact of this tendency is amplified by the distribution of roles at the various institutional levels. The E.U.'s budget cannot be assessed ignoring the functions attributed to these

---

133 Velo, D. (edited by), *L'Europa dei progetti*, op. cit.

various institutional levels. The basic tendency of the federal order becoming outlined in Europe, is a division of roles privileging the directory role for the European institutions and that of providers of services for national institutions and emerging intermediary bodies[134].

The recognition of this tendency is necessarily a first approximation. The distribution of competences and resources at the European Union's various institutional levels will be defined in the course of a gradual process running parallel to the development of economic union.

Subsidiarity is multiplying public, private and public-private intermediary bodies that contribute to providing services of general interest in the broadest possible sense. New means of intervention, not all necessarily financed by the public budget, have multiplied at all the levels at which the European Union is organised[135].

Enhanced cooperation, regulated by the Nice Treaty, is allowing the implementation of initiatives inspired by the integration process and that, *in primis*, contribute to the creation of European industrial and research policies. These initiatives do not affect the community's budget or they do so only to a limited extent. Similar phenomena will appear for structured cooperation as set out by the Lisbon Treaty.

Reference to structured cooperation is extremely significant for this analysis. Structured cooperation was added to treaties specifically in order to allow the development of military cooperation, also with the participation of a restricted number of countries. This form of cooperation could also be extended to other sectors. The fact that it was created so as to return military cooperation between some member countries to within a European framework, immediately allows one to

134 See in this more general perspective the analysis specifically dedicated to a segment of activity by Bottinelli, L., Pavione, E., *Distretti industriali e cluster tecnologici: strategie emergenti di valorizzazione della ricerca e dell'innovazione*, Giuffrè, Milan, 2011.

135 Bruzzi, S., "Impresa comune e perseguimento dell'interesse generale", in *Quaderno della rivista Servizi Pubblici e Appalti*, 2/06.

perceive the originality of the integration process. In the United States, defence spending and funding of research for military reasons is a significant element in the federal budget. Europe is beginning to set up a shared defence, privileging national financing on the basis of a coordinating process.

This research is not aimed at assessing the orientation assumed in terms of its efficiency, effectiveness and lower costs. In this context it is emblematic that the European Union's budget can be significantly unchanged in its organisation and size in the presence of the development of a common defence system[136]. The contrast with the American experience can be fully assessed on the basis of a comparison between the models for a federal state, the American and the European one[137].

The differences in European statehood compared to the American experience, and even more when compared to the experience of traditional national states, has led some to believe that Europe is approaching a breaking point, at which the non-sustainability of the European model for statehood, developed so far by the integration process, will emerge. On the basis of this perspective, economic union and a European defence system will impose greater centralization, resulting in homogenizing the European federal state to experiences of other countries, the United States *in primis*.

---

136 Primavera, S., "Innovazione industriale e prospettive di integrazione nel settore della difesa: verso un mercato UE-USA?", Jean Monnet Interregional Centre of Excellence, Pavia, 2010.

137 The concept of a European army as a peacekeeping force, capable of coordinating with initiatives taken by organisations representing civil society, can be perceived within the framework of these ideas, Papisca, A., "Barack Obama and Herman van Rompuy. New Leadership to educate international politics", *The European Union Review*, 1-2/11.

Those who hold these beliefs consider it essential for the size of the European Union's budget to increase; centralization and a larger federal budget are strictly interdependent phenomena[138].

It is a central issue in this analysis to understand the very foundations on which we base our opinions, which are innovative compared to traditional experiences. One must once again also emphasize that the approach developed is of an interpretative nature and not normative [139].

The fact that it is possible to perceive the option of developing structured cooperation as a strategic choice in order to create a European defence system, for those siding with the option previously referred to, is further confirmation of the fact that an optimal E.U. budget is a problem that cannot be defined a priori, but is instead the consequence of options chosen concerning the manners in which public functions should be implemented within the framework of the Union.

The funding of public services comes after defining the manner in which these services will be organised and implemented.

The more European institutions are assigned a directory role, the more options there are for implementing public services and financing. How should E.U.'s organisation distribute state and public interest roles? What should their charters state and how should their implementation be financed?

---

138 This does not mean coinciding. It is possible to a certain extent to plan an increased budget without affecting the level of centralization and statehood. Allow us to refer to Velo, D., "The European Social Market Economy in the Economic and Monetary Union", *Peace Human Rights*, soon to be published. On the other hand, since it is on a path of continuity with the past, the current evolution is the element adopted to confirm the sustainability of integration's development without the need for significant changes in the size of the Community's budget.

139 This is an indication, deeply-rooted in strategy studies, which, in referring to recently published papers, derives from contributions provided by the Bostonian school. See Porter, M.E., *Competitive advantage*, Free Press, New York, 1985.

A state-controlled organisation founded on subsidiarity puts up for discussion not only the repartition of competence and power between the various institutional levels, from local to European levels, but also puts up for discussion the repartition of competences in the horizontal sense, between operators having diverse characteristics – public, private and state-private – having in common the capability to carry out activities of general interest. This problem has already been addressed in different and in convergent ways applying a variety of theories, with the most important identifiable as federalism, the theory of subsidiarity and the model for a social market economy. These different approaches allow one to understand the various elements of the historical process. Their capacity to develop a cross-fertilisation process can be attributed to the very nature of the ongoing processes involving the change referred to by all the three theories mentioned[140].

For those critically addressing the problem of the Community's budget, these remarks are useful for confirming that we are now observing a change in the very nature of the problem. European statehood is becoming increasingly different when compared to American statehood, with Europe privileging subsidiarity and a social market economy while the United States has experienced increased centralization and social-economic order profoundly influenced by liberism. This divergence is now questioned by the need to develop a profounder integration process between the Atlantic federations. This divergence can be used as an interpretive means for assessing a series of phenomena which have developed in the recent past and are still ongoing. It is this divergence that results in the United States and European budgets being incomparable; it attributes different importance to the various forms with which state or general interest activities can be financed. In this sense it is possible to state that there of no optimal size for an E.U. budget and the same applies to the budgets of all federal

140 Please be so kind as to consult Velo, D., *La grande impresa federale europea. Per una teoria cosmopolitica dell'impresa*, op. cit.

states. Attention at this point moves to the manner in which state activities, and those of general interest, are carried out and to how they are funded[141].

Other considerations can be developed and in turn those summarized in previous pages can be examined and specified in a more analytical manner. What is more important here is that the approach presented can be used to indicate, with sufficient approximation, how an larger European budget is not the only way of strengthening the governing capabilities of European institutions.

In truth, this lack of determinedness is typical of the European integration process. Europe has not implemented a model of state defined by a constitution, but has instead created a new original form of statehood through a gradual constituent process that is both material and formal. It is within this context that one must set the prediction on the basis of which European fiscal federalism and the optimal size of the Union's budget will be defined, following a path of progressive development by stages and on the basis of a script often historicized by the integration process[142].

This flexibility can help the search for shared solutions and this is all the more important when taking into account internationals commitments destined to influence European decision-making processes.

---

141 An orthodox federalist approach will result in hypothesising that the European experience should tend towards adopting the model provided by the United States; a Monet-styled approach would result in the identification of broader areas for an innovative initiative. Aaron, R., Lerner, D., *La querelle de la CED*, Plon, Paris, 1956.

142 AA.VV., *An agenda for a growing Europe*, Oxford University Press, Oxford, 2004.

3.4 Balancing the budget. Formal budgets and material consolidated balance sheets

The ECB is tasked by charter to protect the currency's value. The ESCB's monetary policy must guarantee that inflationist processes are reduced to a minimum; in this sense we have earlier used the expression "neutralization of monetary policy."

The principle of a balanced budget for all institutions, at all levels at which European statehood is organized, is the basis for applying the rules of monetary union to economic union.

The same seems to apply to constitutional rules, in the various sectors to which it is applied, resulting thus in the coherence of plans for a European Monetary and Economic Union, for which there is already a gradual project set in stages with a linearity referring to a project of union perceived ever since the very first phases[143].

Reference to the principle of a balanced budget permits the identification of the object of this analysis only as an initial approximation. Earlier in this chapter we have seen how a series of expenses can be referred to the integration process but not specifically to the E.U. budget.

The "consolidated European budget", drafted by taking into account all activities that can be included in the integration process, *in toto* or in part, as well as their financing, does not coincide with the Community's budget.

At a juridical level the two budgetary concepts are heterogeneous. At government level, a consolidated budget perceived in this manner cannot be the direct responsibility of E.U. institutions. This heteroge-

143 These remarks will require verification since the process is ongoing and therefore subject to risks deriving from contingencies. See methodological considerations by Einaudi, L., "Le premesse del ragionamento economico", *Rivista di Storia Economica*, 3/41.

neity is further confirmed when considering controls of various kinds implemented for public expenditure.

The principle of a balanced budget is usually referred to the budgets of public institutions. The European experience indicates how a series of alternative solutions and instruments can be used for public finalities and those of general interest, without weighing on the budget in the real sense of the word. The problem has become all the more important, since over the years the importance of the Community's budget has become less vital compared to activities linked to the integration process.

When analysing the principle of a balanced budget, one must therefore broaden the perspective to the whole ensemble currently characterised by great heterogeneity. An analysis of the budget in the real sense of the word is an essential part of this investigation, but does not represent the totality of the universe of resources ascribable to public initiatives.

The validity of the balanced budget principle was secondly changed by the rising importance, in state operations, of issues concerning governance rather than the implementation of activities. The very meaning of the principle of a balanced budget changes, as does control over it, when state institutions concentrate their activities on establishing policies and rules, delegating implementation to private or state-private operators.

An empiric approach can link the importance of the principle of a balanced budget to the size of the budget considered. Thus the size of the budget assumes the value of an indicator of the direct role played by state institutions in implementing activities.

These premises once again emphasize the importance of a critical approach, setting the principles affirmed in to a future context, which imposes the need to historicize these principles and leads one to assess their impact differently. Such prudence does not change the importance of the principle of a balanced budget, considered the fundamental rule for the correct organisation of economic union[144].

In historicising the analysis, the first reference is the initial moment at which the principle of regulating the deficits in national budgets was introduced into European Law, consisting in the treaties creating monetary union. Until then the law imposed the E.U.'s budget be balanced, but did not dictate rules for lower constitutional levels.

The treaties that set up European monetary union, established that budgets of member countries must respect the obligation of a deficit no larger than 3%. The treaties specified the medium term objective and the ways in which the deficit should be managed in the presence of adverse or favourable economic trends[145].

These rules must be assessed as the starting point for weighing up the objective of a balanced budget that appeared at a later date. In order to assess this rule and specifically the 3% deficit limit allowed, it is necessary to interrelate this parameter with the economic conditions that prevailed at the time. Such a comparison can contribute to clarifying the context within which this principle assumes meaning[146].

At the historical moment in which the treaties were drafted, the GDP in core-Europe countries moved every year close to an average value of 3%. State investments in turn amounted on average to about 3% of the GDP. Inflation tended to remain below 3%, with not very significant differences between core-Europe countries. The economic system's trends in the European Union's central macro-area resulted in a state deficit equal to or lower than 3% which could be considered

144 Müller-Graff, P.C., "The Treaty of Amsterdam. Characteristics and Perspectives", *The European Union Review*, 2/00.

145 Baimbridge, M. , Whyman, P. (eds), *Fiscal Federalism and European Economic Integration*, Routledge, London, 2004.

146 Bini Smaghi, L., Padoa-Schioppa, T., Papadia, F., "The Transition to EMU in the Maastricht Treaty", *Essays in international finance*, 194/1994.

sustainable and would not lead to tension as far as servicing debt was concerned[147].

Capital accumulated by national communities and its yield in terms of developing national wealth seemed sufficient to deal in real terms with obligations arising from the deficit. This level of deficit was compatible with orthodox monetary management addressed at guaranteeing the currency's value and obliged not to finance the public sector by printing money. This level of deficit was therefore accepted in the treaty that established monetary union.

These considerations are not addressed at defining an optimal configuration of the fiscal policy of economic-monetary union[148]. They are instead aimed at identifying the context in which the restriction to restrict deficits to a 3% maximum was added to treaties in order to establish the historical context defined by this analysis[149].

The parameter involving the maximum deficit allowed must secondly be historicised, also taking into account a number of aspects that are not linked to the economic aspects first considered. A more precise identification of the historical context must necessarily also consider institutional aspects. The restriction to a deficit no larger than 3% refers to the budgets of national member states, an aspect often neglected since traditionally the national aspects of statehood are taken for granted.

In the perspective of the analysis developed here, the national dimension is an element undergoing change. European economic union

---

147 Reference to conditions prevailing in core-Europe correspond to experience acquired in the course of the integration process, which confirmed how all progress made in integration has always respected the condition of being coherent with conditions prevailing in the countries in this macro-area. For a critical analysis see Brumila, A., Buti, M., Franco, D., *The Stability and Growth Pact. The Architecture of Fiscal Policy in EMU*, Palgrave, London, 2001.

148 Musgrave, R.M., *The Theory of Public Finance*, McGraw-Hill, New York, 1959

149 Majocchi, A., "Dallo EMS all'Economic Union e Monetaria: il ruolo della politica fiscale", *Il Federalista*, 1-2/80.

poses the problem of fiscal federalism, and with it that of a harmonious development of multi-level statehood. We will address this aspect in greater depth later on in the book. As far as the problem posed by balanced budgets addressed here is concerned, it emphasizes the importance of taking into account the institutions of individual states. The division of resources available for funding the activities of the institutions that both vertically and horizontally compose the E.U.'s subsidiary order, imposes the need to protect such balance from the risk of modifications caused by deficits unilaterally decided by any institution. The size of the deficit allowed in the budgets of national institutions implies recognition of the level of centralisation that existed when the treaties were ratified. This orientation, as a working hypothesis can be brought back to the persuasion that the deficit could be organised quite easily, envisaging changes in the internal institutional order of a member state.

In truth, changes in the internal institutional order of a member state are destined to affect the qualification of state expenditure and any eventual deficits. A deficit's impact changes depending on the destination of the resources on which the deficit's sustainability depends. A different allocation of resources – and the possibility to generate deficits – between the various institutions of which national statehood is composed, cannot necessarily be considered neutral. There are therefore a number of possible hypotheses that must be empirically assessed.

One reaches similar conclusions when considering the social and more specifically intergenerational elements in the problem. A budget with a deficit transfers the burden deriving from services provided to the current generation to future ones. The 3% maximum bond is based on the idea that this burden placed on future generations will be compensated by the generating of revenue to be enjoyed by these future generations. Such balance cannot exclude the risk of imbalances. This system is also based on the hypothesis of a homogeneity of society's components over time. Should this not be confirmed, relevant implications emerge in terms of social policies. Once again, historicising the decision of maximum deficits allowed, permits one to perceive the implications contributing to a better understanding of the full implications of the decision-making process .

One aspect linked to the social dimension is the increasing importance of standards of living as the objective of state policies - environmental policies, energy policies, new urbanisation models, to mention only a few aspects of this increasingly important trend. The maximum deficit allowed is set within the framework of a quantitative approach that acknowledges a higher GDP as the objective of public policies. When standard of living objectives prevail over that of increasing the GDP, the deficit will no longer be balanced by greater wealth in financial terms; a financial debt cannot be off- set using imponderable, non-financial assets. These considerations support the interpretative hypothesis stating that the limit of a maximum deficit allowed was determined by referring to the various conditions prevailing at the time, without projecting this decision over a long-term perspective in order to take into account predictable innovations with greater economic, social and institutional impact.

These observations identify aspects that demand a critical review of current deficit spending theories.

They pose the problem of a good governance theory capable of updating those inherited from the past[150].

Just as monetary union has neutralized monetary policy, by imposing orthodox currency management, economic union will be able to neutralize deficit spending policies, imposing an orthodox management of public expenditure.

---

150 Einaudi, L., "Il mio piano non è quello di Keynes", *La riforma sociale*, 2/33; Einaudi, L., *Il buongoverno*, Laterza, Bari, 1954; Forte, F., *Luigi Einaudi, il mercato e il buongoverno*, Einaudi, Turin, 1982.

There is a possibility of drafting an innovative economic constitution for the European Union that would provide the basis for achieving economic union[151].

The distinction proposed here between a formal budget and a material consolidated budget derives from the traditional distinction that constitutional law makes between a formal constitution and a material constitution. The two concept are not equal but both find fertile ground for their development within the European integration process. A European material consolidated budget poses problems as far as democratic control is concerned, which has grown in size and importance over time. Enhanced cooperation has permitted the implementation of significant initiatives within the framework of the integration process, with national budgets providing most of the financial burden. Initially these achievements were relatively restricted and of sectorial importance, while nowadays enhanced cooperation could, to a certain extent, be used to address the monetary-financial crisis, mobilizing multiple resources rather than the European budget. It is evident how the problem of democratic legitimization of a constitutional order would emerge and the solutions contained in the Nice Treaty and later in the Lisbon Treaty to provide a legal framework for enhanced cooperation would appear inadequate should this instrument become a founding pillar of the integration process[152].

Economic union will presumably be sanctioned by a treaty as has happened in the past every time a stage in the integration process was completed. One possible alternative solution could consist in a review of the European constitution ratified in the form of the Lisbon Treaty. These two alternatives, which are certainly not equal, could provide

151 Quadrio Curzio, A., *Economisti ed economia per un'Italia europea: paradigmi tra il XVIII e il XX secolo*, Il Mulino, Bologna, 2007.

152 These remarks were written in the spring of 2011. The authors have decided that it would not be appropriate to change them, albeit accepting that events developing while the book was being published, confirm the importance of a careful analysis of this issue.

the framework for providing a constitutional solution to the aforementioned problems.

This confirms the importance that a constitutional regulation of economic union now being developed may assume for the integration process as a whole.

3.5 Welfare reform

In previous pages we mentioned intergenerational problems that demand a critical review of traditional deficit spending policies. This point is of the utmost importance and is better outlined by referring to the link between the principle of a balanced budget and the welfare crisis.

The coinciding of the development of economic-monetary union and a crisis of traditional forms of welfare has occurred for a specific reason. The reference context is provided by the social-economic transformation process that in more developed countries marked the transition from the 20th to the 21st century[153].

The protection of future generations is the state responsibility. This problem is in no way regulated at a constitutional level because in the past intergenerational balance were not a critical issue. In the conditions that matured in the last part of the 20th century, when this protection became a central issue in social-economic policies[154], the constitutional importance of regulating intergenerational relations

---

153 Castles, F.G., *The Future of the Welfare State. Crisis Myths and Crisis Realities*, Oxford University Press, Oxford, 2004.

154 A farsighted analysis of this problem is contained in a report written in the mid-Eighties by C.A. Ciampi, L. Arcuti and A. Longo. This report was circulated at an institutional level.

emerged[155]. The problem lies in an objective of great importance: the definition of laws capable of preventing present generations from creating a deficit resulting in long term debt[156].

The need to reform the welfare system arises firstly from the change there has been in intergenerational relations. The development of intergenerational solidarity was helped in western countries for many decades by a rise in the number of those contributing to the social security system, thus by the significant surpluses held for long periods by Social Security Departments. The Social Security Department registered rises in revenue superior to the rise in the costs they sustained for services rendered. This made the financing of increased forms of solidarity possible, with no apparent burden on future generations. In the Eighties, slower development, deindustrialisation and rising unemployment, a lower birth-rate and the progressive aging of the population, resulted in the emergence of structural imbalances with the inevitable need to reform welfare services[157].

Economic analysis and social-economic policies have had to address the need to privilege organisational aspects rather than economic ones, lengthening the timeframe considered. In a long-term perspective investments became more important than consumption and sustainability became a priority.

The relationship between a balanced budget and welfare reform results in attention focusing on sovereign debt. The economic development experienced by European countries during the post-war period and the growth of welfare fuelled the illusion of the sustainability of structural budget imbalances – within certain limits – and justified in-

155 Buti, M., Franco, D., Pench, L.R., (eds), *The Welfare in Europe. Challenges and Reforms*, Edwar Elgar, Northampton, 1999.

156 For a more in-depth analysis of this problem see Peltzman, G., "Toward a more general Theory of Regulation", *Journal of Law and Economics*, 2/76.

157 Velo D., Velo F., *Ospedali e sviluppo economico*, Angeli, Milan, 2007.

creased sovereign debt as a form of solidarity between generations, within a renewable timeframe devoid of tension.

The illusion has now ended. There is now an increasing awareness that welfare values will only be able to be confirmed with the implementation of a new social-economic order based on good governance and sustainability[158].

3.6 The multi-level budget and the option of resorting to debt

The specific problem that has emerged from our analysis so far concerns whether the development of economic union will affect the budget balancing principle, extending the rules to the different institutions operating within the framework of subsidiarity at both horizontal and vertical levels. One question arising from this approach addresses the issue of whether some institutions can ignore the rule on balanced budgets, while respecting modalities for the exercising of power and for assuming competences[159].

Not all powers have been transferred from national authorities to European institutions but instead to the integration process. The European Union is not organised on the basis of a centralised model adopting previously experimented experiences, but has instead, on each occasion, implemented innovative solutions that have resulted in the de-

---

158 Röpke, W., *La crisi del nostro tempo*, ed. it. Einaudi, Turin, 1946.

159 One example of these statements is the reference to enhanced cooperation, which began to progressively appear in the Sixties and became regulated only a number of decades after starting. During this long period, enhanced cooperation was gradually more precisely outlined thanks to the capability shown by countries part of core-Europe in empirically establishing adequate and evolutionary solutions to address problems that arose in workability. Velo, D. (edited by), *L'Europa dei progetti*, op. cit.

fining of a new form of federal statehood. This process is far from being a completed one and the understanding of possible future configurations of economic union and multi-level budgets can be referred to experiences matured in the history of integration.

One fundamental distinction can be introduced in order to orient the analysis of the nature of processes that could be used to set up a European multi-level budget. On one hand there is the problem posed by the distribution of resources between institutions and the rules to be applied, while on the other there is the problem of the division of public and general interest projects and the rules for regulating them. There is a correlation between these two aspects. What is most important here is the prospect that economic union will redefine institutional order and the responsibility to carry out public duties and those of public interest, not necessarily applying traditional models.

In a perspective of confirming order founded on subsidiarity, economic union will predictably have to address the problem of transferring powers and competences to more bodies – state, private and mixed state-private ones. There will consequently be a need to resolve a complex equation resulting in a differentiated regulation, simultaneously guaranteeing a unitary framework capable of ensuring a convergence of the different solutions applied.

Private, public or state-private bodies will follow different operative logic and it is from this reality that the need for differentiated regulations arises. Public demand and long term investments challenge the decision-making processes, forms of control, and regulations coherent with the nature of activities. These differences must be returned to within a process of united development.

Within the context of globalisation, liberism has established an order that can be chosen as one possible alternative. According to this first option, it is possible to establish a clear distinction between institutions, each responsible for specific functions. By extremely briefly summarizing this position, one can state that according to the liberist approach, public institutions are responsible for public services not ascribable to the markets, while all other activities are the markets' responsibility. This establishes a clear link between the characteristics of an institution and the role it should play. Liberism has reiterated the political-economic order that emerged at the beginning of the industrial revolution, radicalizing a division of roles.

This first option asserted itself at a global level linked to the development of globalisation[160]. It does not correspond to the European experience that has taken place parallel to the development of the integration process. Subsidiarity is the constitutional principle pivotal to European integration. This principle asserted itself progressively, increasingly clearly becoming the anchor point for the organisation of the new stages through which the unification plan was achieved.

Subsidiarity facilitated private and state-private bodies assuming functions of general interest some of which were traditionally the competence of state institutions. Vice versa, this also encouraged state institutions to assume functions traditionally carried out within by markets. In short, subsidiarity allowed the beginning of a reorganisation of social, economic and political systems on the basis of a complex and innovative order capable of adapting to emerging requirements in industrialised countries.

Within the framework of order based on subsidiarity, regulating functions is decisive compared to regulation founded on the nature of the institution implementing them. This is a point of the utmost importance, the understanding of which is often hindered by its apparent simplicity.

So as to embark upon an analysis, in order to understand which rules might allow the creation of economic union complying with the principle of subsidiarity, it is legitimate to formulate an hypothesis.

---

160 Pontifical Council for Justice and Peace, *"Towards reforming the international financial and monetary systems in the context of the global public authority"*, Vatican City, 2011.

In order to define this hypothesis, it is possible to refer to the rules established for monetary union. As seen, these rules can be linked to two fundamental objectives, "zero inflation" and "zero deficit". The "zero debt" principle can be perceived as the third fundamental objective, valid for a number of state activities or those of general interest, following a path of coherent development in order to guarantee respect for the principle of subsidiarity in creating economic union. The Maastricht Treaty set limits to deficits and to sovereign debt. The debate, of constitutional importance, that developed when the possibility of creating economic union emerged, immediately addressed the possibility of lowering the level of deficit allowed. The hypothesis envisaged here, to be assessed and more precisely defined, envisages that abolishing the option of being able to resort to sovereign debt is the logical evolution of the federal order currently implemented.

The neutralization of financial policies envisaged, imposes first of all more specific outlining as far as the activities to which it would be applied are concerned. The fundamental conflict is between consumption and investments. The restrictions applied to the financing of public spending without resorting to debt has a specific constitutional objective, that of avoiding imposing on future generations the costs linked to money spent on the current generation. This same principle can be outlined in economic-financial terms as preventing debt being used to finance expenditure that will not produce sufficient revenue to repay the debt itself.

Principles of good governance applied to investments do not imply the neutralization of the option of resorting to debt, but rather guarantee the financial balance of operations. Investments are called upon to generate value in order to pay off the funding obtained.

In theory, the border between these two categories of expenditure is relatively well-defined. There is an intermediate area, consisting of investments that can have positive effects on the system without generating revenue in order to establish a direct link between costs and revenue in a strictly financial sense[161]. Since this analysis is addressed at defining a general theory, in order to provide initial orientation when faced with change that could be of significant importance, we do not consider it legitimate on this occasion to address the multitude of declinations that can be assumed by investments of general interest. In our opinion, it seems more important to understand to what extent and in what way the aforementioned border between expenditure and investments can be defined, referring to an economic union's constitutional order.

The distinction between expenditure and investments can attenuate when the two activities merge in the budget of an institution called upon to develop activities addressed at both the short and long term. The rigour of this distinction is destined to conflict with the unitary vision each institution develops as far as its own activities are concerned[162].

These reflections have been developed more organically by the cultural traditions of business economics; the firm is considered as an institution restricted by a unifying perspective of individual activities[163]. This suggests that a solution to the problems addressed should be searched for through a form of organisation dividing expenditure and revenue possibly between different institutional subjects.

In summary, this outline leads one to set out, as a very first approximation, an organisational draft for economic union that would on one hand have activities addressed at expenditure of general interest, bound by the neutralisation of debt incurred by state institutions, and on the other activities aimed at investments of general interest linked

161 This problem has been addressed in depth by P. Saraceno at a theoretical level and with empiric reference to the experience of Italian state-owned companies. See Saraceno, P., *Il sistema delle imprese a partecipazione statale nell'esperienza italiana*, Giuffrè, Milan, 1975; Vaccà, S., "Pasquale Saraceno: studioso di politica industriale", in *Economia e Politica industriale*, 72/91.

162 Caselli, L., *L'impresa pubblica nell'economia di mercato*, Giuffrè, Milan, 1970.

163 Usai, G., *Le imprese*, Giuffrè, Milan, 2007.

to the need to respect financial balance, carried out by autonomous institutions be they state institutions, private ones or state-private owned.

Such organisation would effectively result in the principle of financial neutralisation based on the activities undertaken.

This idea cannot be seen as a rigid model; it is a preliminary one and can be used to historicise the "zero sovereign debt" objective envisaged earlier as the third fundamental rule for the economic-monetary union currently planned by the European Union.

There is an important precedent confirming the aforementioned method. In the United States, federally-owned companies were an innovative form of public businesses obliged to respect financial balance. This form of federal public companies was created during the New Deal and continues to be used for priority objectives mainly in defence and research . Federal Government Corporations are created using federal laws but do not appear in the federal budget as a direct consequence of their autonomy[164]. This regulation has close points of contact with the order outlined above, so as to restrict the framework within which financial neutralisation can be applied.

The experience of Federal Government Corporations returns one to the analysis presented above and founded on the distinction between the European budget and the integration process' consolidated budget. In the United States' case too there are budgets that are not the responsibility of the federal budget but that of federal initiatives. In more general terms, those oriented at reconstructing the material constitution, should take into account aspects of reality that have not yet been bestowed with formal juridical status[165]. The importance of re-

---

164 Primavera, S., "L'esperienza americana delle Federal Government Corporations. Spunti di riflessione per la grande impresa federale europea", in Velo, D. (edited by), *L'Europa dei progetti*, op. cit.

165 It is in this perspective that one should also consider the problem of the role played by democratic institutions in being a reference point in decision-making

marks referring to the budget can be broadened, setting the budget problem within the context of the integration process, considered as a whole and as its various expressions.

This analysis identifies two fundamental variables in addressing the problems of a multi-level budget and the option of resorting to debt.

The first variable is the definition of a multi-level budget assigning responsibilities and resources to the institutions in which the union is organised, following a vertical subsidiary order. Budgets defined in this manner could be under strict restrictions as far as the option of resorting to debt is concerned. It is in this context that interrelations between fiscal federalism and financial neutralisation of state expenditure are set.

The second variable is the definition of state, private or state-private operators able to assist the institutions, typically in a horizontal subsidiary order, so as to implement activities and investments of general interest, with operational logic based on economic-financial responsibility and balance. These bodies will be free to resort to debt on condition they do not resort to issuing bonds guaranteed by state institutions.

This theory identifies two totally distinct axes. The current outlook identifies many cases that don't place themselves in one or the other axis. It is sufficient to refer to institutions that resort to debt in order to finance medium and long-term investments, capable of generating sufficient financial resources to service debt. These investments respect the basic rules described here, but are not set within the framework of a division of competences on the bases of the two aforementioned options. This simple example emphasizes how the approach described here is useful for outlining an orientation, a starting

---

processes concerning their areas of competence. Matarazzo, R. (edited by), *Democracy in the EU after the Lisbon Treaty*, Edizioni Nuova Cultura, Rome, 2011.

point, aimed at finally defining a rigorous plan for a economic union's multi-level budget.

The integration process has always implemented innovative solutions, respecting a number of basic rules that have guaranteed continuity within the process itself. It is the concept of "evolutionary compromise" that identifies the capability to innovate, while respecting existing conditions, creating realistic solutions able to evolve towards increasingly advanced equilibriums[166].

The layout of the analysis presented here is based on a renewed idea of state-private relations and, ultimately, results is considering all operators as institutions forming an order set up on the basis of subsidiarity, in which various categories of institutions are called upon to respect rules that are appropriate for their nature, be they state, private or state-private[167]. Such order is coherent with a social market economy as organised in the past and as evolving in current conditions.

These observations indicate that the definition of a multi-level budget, and from another perspective also fiscal federalism, in this phase implies not so much a exercise in identifying practical solutions, but the need to understand the determinants of future institutional and social-economic order. The crucial problem that cannot be avoided is that of rules to be respected by all subjects involved in the transformation, be they already operational or new to the vast area of activities of general interest.

Two fundamental rules have already been established and are being introduced; currency management protecting its value and the balancing of state budgets. The third rule, which emerges from this analysis, is debt regulation, destined to assume the form of neutralizing financing

166 The words "evolutionary compromise" are not part of the lexicon used by Jean Monnet, but certainly portray his tendency to historicize the principle of responsibility. Monnet, J., *Mémoires*, op. cit.

167 Velo, D., *L'impresa federale europea. Per una teoria cosmopolitica dell'impresa*, op. cit.; Forte, F,. Felice, F. (eds), *Il liberalismo delle regole*, op. cit.

for operations unable to create financial flows equal to the investment and the form of good governance for investments able to be serviced thanks to financial flows generated. The coming constituent debate will address the issue of whether these two different categories of activities, albeit sharing the objective of serving the general interest and respecting the balance, should be the competence of different institutions, obliged to respect the rules and answer to controls based on the their activities.

Should the orientation outlined here be considered valid, it will certainly be necessary to overcome the dualism adopted so far in defining vertical subsidiarity.

In the current conditions, the European Commission must respect the zero deficit and zero debt constraints, while at the moment neither of these rules have to be respected by lower level national and regional institutions. In order to overcome this dualism, two alternative options have already emerged, both still to be defined but already clearly oriented at achieving the opposite. A first solution has centralizing or national-European characteristics. It is aimed at providing European institutions with the same freedom enjoyed by lower-level institution, both regarding deficit spending and the option of issuing public debt. A second solution is of a federal nature and is aimed at extending to a national and regional level the constraints that must currently be respected by European Institutions.

This second alternative corresponds to a vision of Europe as the workshop for a new form of statehood, with a first requirement addressed at clarifying the manner in which forms of financing development are to be envisaged in this context.

3.7 Financing development: the Tennessee Valley Authority model

The solutions outlined in the previous paragraph are certainly functional to the objective of achieving balance. Their effectiveness could be minor in achieving other objectives, *in primis* a balanced development of the system. It is possible to envisage that in some areas it may be difficult to organise institutions capable of sustaining development with investments capable of guaranteeing sufficient financial revenue. The characteristics of less developed areas may require more risky investments made with a more long term perspective and harder to finance by resorting to markets. The relative underdevelopment of some areas may result in the need to import entrepreneurial and managerial skills from other areas, which would not be in line with the principles of territorial autonomy. Other phenomena may obstruct balanced development, as economic theory has shown.

There is a precedent that can contribute to clarifying this point. During the Thirties, in order to overcome the underdevelopment of the Tennessee Valley, the Roosevelt administration invented a new form of intervention, creating an authority with one specific task. This marked the beginning of an innovative form of development policy based on the convergence of public objectives and a means capable of respecting market rules[168]. The instrument capable of reconciling these two objectives, as mentioned above, was the creation of a federal authority. This form of intervention was later developed with the creation of Federal Government Corporations, as mentioned in the previous paragraph.

Before analysing the experience of the Tennessee Valley Authority (TVA), it is necessary to emphasize that we are not envisaging that a repetition of this experience, following the same rules, could be a applied to the creation of European economic union. America's New

168 Shonfield, A., *Il capitalismo moderno. Mutamenti nei rapporti tra potere pubblico e privato*, ed. it. ETAS Kompass, Milan, 1967.

Deal contributed to an increased centralisation of power, and should Europe wish to protect the cornerstone constitutional principle of subsidiarity, there would be the problem in appointing federal authorities respectful of the European federal structure, characterized by far less centralised governance than the United States.

This reference is an initial interpretation of the TVA's activities which will be outlined later on[169].

There is a second aspect that must be specified to better understand the topicality of the TVA's experience from the current European perspective. Leaving aside the specific forms assumed by this authority, one must emphasize how it was called upon to contribute to the country's development within a context in which federal state expenditure was obliged to respect a balanced budget.

This aspect must be specified since it does not correspond to the vision set out by many economic schools of thought seeing Roosevelt's New Deal as validation of Keynesian deficit spending strategies.

The launching of Roosevelt's New Deal preceded the spreading of Keynesian policies. During the Thirties, the American federal government was still obliged to respect a balanced budget. The importance of this aspect must be underlined in order to better assess the topicality of the TVA experience from the perspective of the current European Union[170].

---

169 In this way the experience of the United States assumed the importance of significant precedent, not that of a model to be faithfully replicated. In the Italian tradition one should remember the contribution provided by Saraceno, who learned a great deal from the American New Deal so as to outline industrial development policies for the Italian reconstruction. Rullani, E., "Pasquale Saraceno: un industrialista al servizio della politica di sviluppo", *Nuova Fase. Quaderni di cultura e politica sociale*, 2/95; Velo, F., "I piani europei e la ricostruzione delle città italiane nel secondo dopoguerra. Sviluppo sociale, economico, industriale", in AA.VV., *Guerra, monumenti, ricostruzione*, Marsilio, Venice, 2011.

170 A historical revision of the theories that have stated how the New Deal owed a lot to Keynesian theories in underway. On this subject see Felisini, D., *Inseparabili: lo Stato, il mercato e l'ombra di Colbert*, Rubbettino, Soveria Mannelli, 2010. This

During the Thirties, there was a turning point in the development of modern capitalism in the United States. New forms of organisation occurred in companies implementing the so-called managerial revolution. Markets were regulated by federal legislation that profoundly changed the manner in which they worked. Within this framework, the creation of the Securities and Exchange Commission marked the most significant reform. New models of industrial development emerged, modifying traditional public-private relations. It was in this specific context that the new economic institution activated by the Roosevelt administration, the federal authority was set, operating autonomously in developing an activity of general interest and respecting rules involving economic-financial balance.

The TVA was the best known federal authority, both due to the innovation in the solutions adopted and the size of intervention capable of affecting social-economic balance in a number of states part of the Tennessee Valley macro-region, becoming a symbol of the New Deal.

The TVA was created in 1933 with the objective of re-launching the area with an initiative working on various fronts. The measures adopted involved industrial policies, agricultural policies, the police force and social policies, consisting of an organic approach in order to achieve governance capabilities the states involved were unable to guarantee[171].

Federal intervention is correctly understood in current publications as an innovative example of regional policy and the assessment

current historical revision suggests a "heretical" interpretation on the basis of which the Keynesian deficit spending policies adopted by the Unites States were the seed that caused the American and international crisis that exploded in the last 25 years of the 20th Century.

171 The Tennessee Valley covers seven States, at the time all characterised by a degree of economic-industrial underdevelopment. This would change as a direct consequence of federal intervention.

parameters used are therefore of an economic nature[172]. In our analysis it is more important to analyse this experience on the basis of its constitutional importance. The creation of this federal authority provided a new instrument for governing the Union, changing the United States' economic constitution.

The legislation creating this authority established the foundations for the good governance of the initiative. The measures adopted should be historicised referring to the environment and the times. The underlying logic derives from a long term prospect that remains important as an example. The most important measures adopted can be summarised as follows. Managerial powers were highly centralised. The TVA was led by a board of three directors appointed by the president of the United States, respectively with a three, six and nine year mandate, in order to guarantee gradual change-over and continuity. Management had to respect transparency and economic-financial balance criteria and the Authority was called upon to report to the president and to Congress on their work and their results. The charter envisaged the possibility that the TVA could resort to financial markets, respecting an established limit[173], issuing bonds guaranteed by the federal government. The Authority was also expected to rigorously respect its responsibilities in guaranteeing financial balance.

Measures contained in its constituent deed identify, albeit not fully, the innovative nature of this initiative. The TVA is a state institution but one obliged to respect management rules characterising private enterprise, *in primis* the obligation to respect economic-financial balance. The TVA is a state-owned company that differs radically

172 See also Bruzzi, S., *Impresa pubblica, sviluppo industriale e mezzogiorno: l'attualità della lezione di Pasquale Saraceno*, Jean Monnet Interregional Centre of Excellence, Pavia, 2011.

173 The charter establishes a $50 million limit which at the time was adequate for financing a short to medium term strategic plan. During the years that followed, thanks to the initiative's success, the TVA was supported by the federal government in expanding its activities.

from all previous models in which state intervention was perceived as being outside the market. The TVA is obliged to repay funding received from the federal government, while traditional state-owned companies could envisage that resources received from the state were non-repayable. These measures turned out to be extremely effective. The distribution of roles between the federal government and the TVA became increasingly clear and were consolidated following quite a long start-up period.

The federal government drafted a strategy coherent with regional development, in a long term perspective not compatible with the typical timeframe used for business activities. Risks were covered by a series of long-term loans considered appropriate for developing activities.

The TVA developed an efficient and effective economic administration, achieving levels of competitiveness equal to those of private companies operating in the same sector. The balanced budget constraints and the repayment of loans oriented decision-making processes towards good business governance.

This resulted in an innovative convergence between objectives of general interest and market tools. The TVA represented a new form of state-private relations destined to become increasingly rooted in industrialised countries over the following decades[174].

This innovative state-private relationship is at the basis of the TVA's success, with the company achieving high levels of profitability and high external revenue. At an industrial level the TVA has gradually become one the largest producers of electrical energy in the United States, increasingly financing its own development while simultaneously reducing its need for federal funding. The TVA's contribution to the territory's development can be measured by the rise in

---

174 Velo, D., *L'impresa federale europea. Per una teoria cosmopolitica dell'impresa*, op. cit.

the average income of citizens residing in the region[175]. This same innovative relationship was destined to give rise to a widespread debate opposing innovators and conservatives. This debate had important effects on the Authority's development. This point is significant for better understanding the overall lessons to be learned from this experience.

On one hand, for its development programmes the TVA was able to rely on the support of innovators, more inclined to assess the expansion of state-owned and state-private companies without preconceptions, and also more specifically in favour of expanding the role played by public institutions in the American economy. On the other hand, the TVA was obliged to face growing opposition from some conservatives and in particular from more radical liberists[176].

After the war this conflict resulted in the Eisenhower administration reducing and then abolishing federal financial support for the TVA. For the Authority this decision marked both a moment of crisis and an opportunity for strategic renewal. In 1959 the TVA's charter was changed following a lengthy and broad debate, establishing the TVA's full autonomy, the option to resort to the market was recognised has being without limitations as a direct consequence of state guarantees being abolished, and the repayment of federal investments received was also approved. A territorial constraint was added in order to avoid distortions of competitiveness in favour of the TVA, ascrib-

175 This measure should be considered a first approximation since the rise in income is certainly linked to a series of additional causes, including the TVA's positive impact. Between 1933 and 1953 the average income for the areas in which the TVA operated rose from 44% to 51% in the national average. This data is all the more significant when taking into account the rise in the American GDP for the same period. See Bruzzi, S., *Impresa pubblica, sviluppo industriale e mezzogiorno*, op. cit.

176 The two large political-cultural groups described here with the words innovators/conservatives is generally understood as referring to opposition between Democrats and Republicans. In the United States political-cultural alignments have traditionally been characterized by a broad heterogeneity and thus all simplifications are acceptable only as an approximation.

able *in primis* to federal funding received in earlier years, with the Authority bound to only operate within the geographical area for which development had been planned.

The crisis that arose from the federal administration's liberist decisions therefore resulted in a renewal of the TVA's entrepreneurial model, thereby strengthening the Authority itself. The charter approved in the years of the New Deal already stated the public company's responsibility obliging management to implement good company governance. The measures adopted by the Eisenhower administration strengthened this position even more, contributing to encourage the Authority to improve the quality of its services, increasing its own competitiveness. It was on these foundations that the initiative's success increased on the internal American market. On this same basis, at an international level the TVA became an example of a model of a successful state-owned company that operates respecting the market's rules. The TVA represents a real liberalism model of a state-owned company antithetic to a statist vision and equally antithetic to the liberist vision[177].

The TVA has proved that it is possible to set up an activity of general interest in an innovative manner while respecting the rules of good governance. This experience assumes additional importance as a good example when one considers that the TVA has confirmed its continuity within a competitive context characterised by radical change. This alone is enough to prove the historical importance of this experience. Initially it was possible to assess the TVA as an exceptional form of intervention, destined to be overcome once the problem that justified its creation

177 One must remember the distinction made in previous pages between liberalism and liberism. The American culture underestimated this distinction as proven by the fact that its vocabulary does not distinguish between these two concepts; empirically, this distinction is found in a number of experiences, among them that of the TVA.

was resolved. Its success over time has proved the potential of the new model for state-owned companies that appeared[178].

In order to assess the change experienced by the TVA in 1959, one must also underline one further aspect. The Authority was created as decided by the federal administration, which also established the rules and the operational system to be followed in developing its activity. The 1959 crisis demanded instead that the TVA should address a change in the federal administration's outlook and regulate a renewal of its strategies on the basis of its own autonomous initiative and own capabilities. Using an evocative image, one can state that the United States Federal Government's new outlook, which changed from liberalism to liberism, in 1959 obliged the TVA to go against the trend so as to reaffirm its legitimacy, while during the New Deal it was instead a direct expression of Roosevelt's neo-liberalist plans.

Having overcome this critical moment, in the years that followed the TVA progressively lost its emblematic importance, since the Sixties and the decades that followed were characterised by a problem that was easier to resolve such as the correct management of a consolidated business success in a mature sector such as the production of hydro-electric energy.

Once again, one aspect of the law approved in 1959 provided the TVA with an opportunity to renew its development in a positive manner, transforming a constraint contained in this new legislation into an opportunity.

As mentioned, this legislation limited the Authority's activities by restricting the territory within which it was permitted to operate to the Tennessee Valley. The clearly stated objective of this law was to avoid a distortion of competition in the United States' internal market. This law led the TVA to intensify its relations with the territory, contribut-

---

178 The development and success of Federal Government Corporations, previously mentioned, supports these statements. See Primavera, S., "L'esperienza americana delle Federal Government Corporations", op. cit.

ing in ensuring that the reference regions participated in the development that characterised the entire United States system during the Sixties and Seventies.

A capability to support local industrial development should be firstly identified with the favourable tariffs the TVA could demand for supplying electricity. This experience does not differ greatly from the success achieved in France by the state-owned EDF. There are different characteristics, but are both competitive state-owned companies that play a role in the energy sector[179].

The link between the TVA and economic development in the areas in which it operates *de facto* established regional policies also in the years that followed, even if this is not formally acknowledged, since it had by then become an aspect inherent in a consolidated order. Ultimately, the TVA's role in terms of regional policy during that period no longer emerges since the Authority's success permitted the self-funding of its development without resorting to federal funds allocated to balanced territorial development.

The political economic system's lack of perception did not effectively prevent the TVA from continuing to play a positive role in the system's balanced development[180].

179 Mosconi, F., "The Age of European Champions. A new Chance for EU Industrial Policy", in *The European Union Review*, 1/06. The parallel that can be made in some aspects between the American and the French state-owned companies refers to the role played by J. Monnet, first as Roosevelt's advisor and then as the creator of the French Commissariat au Plan after the war.

180 The fact that failures are perceived with greater evidence than successes can be considered physiological, to the extent that no need for corrective decision-making processes emerges.

3.8 Financing development: the European Investment Bank model

The Tennessee Valley Authority is a model of a state-owned company the activity of which if addressed at objectives of general interest and with its management bound to respect principles of an economic character as well as efficiency and effectiveness. This results in resorting to debt becoming a positive element since it guarantees the use of resources to make socially useful investments also capable of generating sufficient revenue for repaying loans.

This experience is comparable to that of the European Investment Bank (EIB) which was based on the same fundamental principles as the TVA, in a different sector, the banking one.

This experience is of particular importance within the framework of our analysis, since it allows one to verify whether equivalent rules can be applied to different fields of activity, such as the industrial sector, services, banking and others, so as to establish a coherent order. Ultimately, the problem addressed here is the definition of methods and rules that are coherent with the implementation of a social market economy capable of guaranteeing balanced development, within a constitutional framework set up on the basis of the principle of subsidiarity.

The EIB was created in 1958 as an instrument for supporting the integration process within the context of general interests and the rules established by the Treaty of Rome. The new institution found itself operating in a still fragmented European capital market as far as the banking system and financial markets were concerned. A lack of capital and the market's relative inefficiency left the EIB ample space for affirming its role. This relative advantage helped consolidate the institution's position and in the years that followed it proved itself capable of playing a leading role amidst increasing competitiveness from other intermediaries[181].

Ever since it was founded, the EIB assumed specific characteristics confirmed in the course of its later development. This is the most important aspect addressed here.

From the day it was founded, the EIB assumed as its primary and principle mission the task of working side by side with the state on economic matters, as an alternative means of increasing the state budget and the use of emergency budgets addressing state expenditure. Direct state intervention in the economy is, generally speaking, aimed at guaranteeing a supply of goods and services that markets are unable to provide. The EIB is set within this context as an institution oriented at guaranteeing supply in specific areas of general interest, restricted by its charter, and respecting rigorous management rules. Both aspects are important, the sectors of activity and the rules of conduct.

The correlation between areas of activity and rules of conduct is called upon to guarantee the achievement of objectives of general interest without distorting market conditions. In order to ensure this would be possible, the EIB needed to ensure it conformed with competitiveness regulations. One must emphasize how this approach anticipated by decades shared intervention addressed at the creation of a single market, extending and rendering increasingly coherent the European regulation of state intervention in the economy.

These observation are better defined when first taking into account a number of the more important rules the EIB is obliged to respect.

In primis, the EIB is not permitted to provide "below cost" financing, more precisely financing at interest rates that systematically differ from those offered by markets. Should the bank consider it ap-

181 Harrop, J., *An Evaluation of the European Investment Bank: prospect and retrospect*, SUERF Series, 23/78; Nardi, F., Pontolillo, V., Tresoldi, C., *Gli investimenti industriali ed il loro finanziamento tramite gli istituti di credito speciale*, Banca d'Italia, Rome, 1973.

propriate to ignore this rule, each operation must be justified to governing authorities. The bank must carry out rigorous preliminary investigations so as to assess the merit of the credit, respecting consolidated assessment criteria adopted by the banking system. Respecting this rule is essential for good governance of the EIB; it also results in avoiding the risk that the bank will replace financing offered by private competitors by exploiting its privileged position. The EIB is called upon to integrate the activities of national banking systems implementing operations that would otherwise not be financed.

One must emphasize how these rules contribute to extending the EIB's good governance to the subject financed. The default of state intervention in the credit sector, as observed in various cases, consist in the an overlapping of decision-making criteria typical of the state operator with decision-making criteria in the private banking system. The result of this overlap could be the imbalance of the state credit intermediary and encouragement given to those receiving financing to implement less rigorous management. This would mean that economic balance as the primary rule of all economics would not have been respected.

The EIB presented a tendency that was the symmetric opposite, consisting of the adoption of decision-making criteria typical of the private banking sector to implement operations involving objectives of general interest. This provides state initiatives with effectiveness.

This is fundamental point of contact between the TVA and the EIB. The TVA outlined a new form of state-owned competitive company, while the EIB outlined a new model for a competitive state-owned bank. In both cases the word competitive refers to market principles and good governance rules, adopted in both cases to implement projects of general interest.

As far as the fields of activity in which the EIB has been authorised to operate, one must acknowledge that the original charter has been maintained, setting out its implementation on the basis of changes made within the economic system.

The Treaty of Rome assigned the EIB with a role involving support for the creation of the European Community and the bank was called upon by the treaty to contribute to balanced development[182].

The object of the EIB's activities was not identified as restricted to one specific sector or a defined series of specialisations, nor was the bank's activity restricted to a specific territorial region. The object of the EIB's activities was set out as a mission with political-economic characteristics, such as contributing to the balanced development of the European Community. This allowed the bank to renew its activities based in the European Community's development as well as changes in the economic-social context. The continuity of guideline criteria did not prevent a continuous evolution, also involving important changes, of the admissibility of the investments to financing. It was possible for the objective of a balanced development to be pursued over time only on condition that activities were renewed to ensure they were achieved[183].

Initially the EIB's activities concentrated on financing regional development and projects that were of interest to a number of member states. Both these sectors of the market were inadequately served by the banking system; the first due to a lack of short term appeal, the second because it did not coincide with the national dimension that at the time characterised individual banking systems that were not yet integrated.

The geographical areas in which the EIB was permitted to intervene to finance regional development changed progressively, parallel to economic change in each area. Later on the territorial rules experienced drastic change when the integration process began to expand, from the six founding countries to the current 27 member states. New member states presented new problems to the bank's core business,

182 On this see Article 130 of the Treaty of Roma. An in-depth analysis of this problem is provided by Gilbert, P., Greppi, E., Marchegiani, G., Ratti, G., *La Banca Europea per gli Investimenti*, Pirola, Milan, 1991.

183 Vilain, D., "La réglementation des placements est-elle vraiment contraignante?", in *Revue d'economie financiére*, 11/89.

and new development strategies became necessary to address social-economic issues with specific characteristics[184]. The adaptation process, determined by the enlargement and deepening of the integration process, never questioned the EIB's role as an instrument in European regional politics[185].

Similar observations apply to the qualification of projects of common interest for a group of member states. Initially this sector of activity could be described, with sufficient approximation, as a residual area not served by national banking systems. During the early years of the bank's activities, financing was concentrated on specific projects, assessed individually, but unlikely candidates for financing from national banks on the basis of traditional assessment criteria.

An evolutionary tendency developed later on, running parallel to the development of shared European policies. Transport policies[186], the creation of an integrated network of infrastructures of European importance, energy policies, environmental policies, industrial and research policies developed gradually in innovative ways and not always following linear processes. The development of common policies is a process that is still fully underway, destined to always identify new contents and new configurations. Enhanced cooperation, already discussed in previous pages, has contributed to outline in a totally original manner a number of common policies within the integration process; enhanced cooperation is an exemplary case in this analy-

184 European Investment Fund, *Jeremie. Joint European Resources for Micro to Medium Enterprises Progress Report on Evaluation and Implementation Activities in 27 EU Member States*, European Investment Bank, Luxembourg, 2007.

185 Commission of the European Communities, *Communication from the Commission to the European Parliament, the Council, the European Economic and Social Committee and the Committee of the Regions. Cohesion Policy: Strategic Report 2010 on the Implementation of the Programmes 2007-2013*, Commission of the European Communities, Brussels, 2010.

186 Directorate-General Mobility and Transport, *Mid-term Review of the 2007-2013 TEN-T Multi Annual Work Programme Project Portfolio*, Commission of the European Union, Brussels, 2010.

sis for understanding how the EIB's activities were called upon to be part of change processes with extremely innovative characteristics.

The idea of contributing to a balanced development of the European Community, and later the European Union, led to an expansion of the EIB's activities to new sectors that also had in common that they were an expression of European economic policies addressed at balanced development[187].

During the Eighties the EIB began to operate in the energy sector. In the Nineties the bank was authorised to intervene in a new priority area, destined to assume growing importance over the years, and consisting in environmental protection. Alongside the development of European industrial policies supporting key sectors, the EIB began to finance investments in technological innovation.

The EIB's traditional policies regarding infrastructures resulted in significant intervention in the new-generation infrastructure sector, *in primis* telecommunications[188]. The fall of the Berlin Wall and the consequent entry of Eastern European country in the European Union provided the bank with an opportunity to expand its activities, both in the sense geographical areas covered and in the kind of intervention implemented.

---

187 Becker, M., *La banque européenne d'investissement*, La Documentation Française, Paris, 1973; Mosconi, F., *La Banque Européenne d'Investissement*, Centre de Recherches Européennes, Lausanne, 1977.

188 The development of new areas of intervention were accompanied by the approval of innovative means of financial intervention. The Jessica, Jeremie, Elena and TEN-T programmes are examples of this. See Commission of the European Communities, *Jessica: Ioint European Support for Sustainable Investment in City Areas*, Commission of the European Communities, Brussels, 2006; Commission of the European Communities, *Jeremie: a Joint Regio-EIF-EIB Initiative Supporting Improved Access to Finance for EMSs*, Commission of the European Communities, Brussels, 2006; Commission of the European Communities, Directorate-General Environment, *Policy News: Elena Supports Cities and Regions in Developing Sustainable Solutions*, Commission of the European Communities, Brussels, 2010; European Investment Bank, *The Loan Guarantee Instrument for Trans-European Transport Network Projects*, EIB, Luxembourg, 2008.

Starting at the end of the Nineties, the bank's activities were positively influenced by an increased availability of structural funds provided by the European Commission and this allowed an expansion of interventions coordinated between the EIB and the Commission itself[189].

More recent activities have allowed the EIB's role as an institute specialised in structural interventions of a micro-economic nature to become entrenched and strengthened[190]. This reasserted and updated the basic characteristics on which the institute itself was founded, and more specifically a capability to reconcile objectives of general interest with economic management respectful of the principles of competitiveness[191].

In the course of its evolution the EIB assumed the role of a model, as happened with the TVA, to be referred to avoid distorting state intervention in the economy. The importance of the aforementioned models can be fully appreciated taking into account alternative and distorting models that failed for these very reasons. Italy's experience with the Cassa per il Mezzogiorno (Fund for the South) and state participation is emblematic in a negative sense[192].

---

189 European Commission, Directorate-General for Internal Policies, *The Implications of EIB and EBRD Co-financing for the EU Budget*, European Parliament, Brussels, 2011.

190 See the EIB's annual reports, exemplary in pursuing the objective of transparency in the public communication of its activities.

191 Sironi Mariotti, M, *Banca Europea per gli Investimenti. I finanziamenti integrativi*, Istituto di Studi Politici e Amministrativi, Verona, 1982; Bermejo, R., "La Banque Européenne d'investissement", in *Revue Internationale de Droit économique*, 1/88.

192 An economist from the Roman School, for a long time involved with the EIB, has provided an effective summary of this institute's characteristics understanding the radical differences with other institutes specialised in financing development.

"The European economy has entered a phase of profound structural adjustments (...) The EIB is deeply committed to facilitating and promoting these changes, not only by simply providing credit to initiatives that deserve from a business and sectorial perspective, but also by providing technical, financial and economic advice, so that "quantity" (the allocation of sufficient amounts of money

3.9 Lesson learned from a failure: the Cassa per il Mezzogiorno (Fund for the South)

President Roosevelt's advisors involved in the New Deal included Rosenstein-Rodan, who played an important role. His contribution was of particular importance in creating the TVA and more in general United States regional policies for the period considered.

Rosenstein-Rodan's theory was based on a fundamental principle. According to this economist, backward areas experience a structural imbalance, consisting in a lack of resources for financing development as well as an excessively large workforce. This approach must be historicised. At the time development coincided with the transition from an economy based on agriculture to the beginning of industrialisation. The thesis at the centre of Rosenstein-Rodan's analysis was that this structural imbalance could only be overcome through state intervention capable of affecting existing balance and sparking change processes[193].

This theory derived from Rosenstein-Rodan's experience matured in the course of the New Deal[194].

---

capable of ensuring an investment project gets off the ground and attracts other financiers) and "quality" (providing flexible financial solutions also suited to the project itself, and with them suggestions and information addressed at improving effectiveness) fuel one another. Following in the footsteps of the best European banking traditions, the EIB does not perceive itself as a third financier in search of mere financial revenue to be gained in as short a time as possible to then move on to other initiatives more or less set within a coherent plan, but as a stable partner bringing far vaster and diversified interests and above all concerned about the success of the investment in the interest of promoting the economy in general", Izzo, L., "Presentazione", in AA.VV., *La Banca Europea per gli Investimenti*, Pirola, Milan, 1991, pp. 1-2.

193 Rosenstein-Rodan, P.N., *Programming in Theory and in Italian Practice*, MIT, Boston, 1955.

194 Chandler, L.V., *America's Greatest Depression, 1929-1941*, Harper & Row, New York, 1970; Romasco, A.U., *Roosevelt's New Deal. The Politics of Recovery*, Oxford University Press, Oxford, 1983.

In the post-war period, he addressed the problem of repeating the success of American regional policies applying similar solutions to underdeveloped European areas, among them, *in primis*, southern Italy. This attempt was not a success. The Italian government acted in a different manner and this failure is filled with lessons, specifically regards to the problems addressed in this book. Rosenstein-Rodan's attempt to repeat the American experience applying it to underdeveloped European areas clashed with a first obstacle of an institutional nature. In the case of the New Deal, the states in the Tennessee River area benefitted from federal initiatives and financing. At the time there existed no form of federation in Europe and no European institution capable of providing any form of governance – if not a government – that would be effective in the countries that could potentially benefit from such intervention.

In order to overcome this obstacle, Rosenstein-Rodan envisaged the creation of a state institution, in the form of a trust or company, owned 50% by more developed countries and 50% by European countries with underdeveloped areas. This was an hypothesis of a confederal nature with the joint participation of financing countries and countries benefitting from intervention in order to make both groups of countries co-responsible.

This approach was conceived by Rosenstein-Rodan with a general perspective for all underdeveloped areas in less industrialised European countries and would guide the economist's initiatives aimed specifically at the Italian situation.

A second obstacle faced by Rosenstein-Rodan in his attempt to apply to Italy the experience matured in the Unites States' New Deal consisted of the traditions that had become entrenched in the Italian social-economic system over previous decades. Italy had already set out its own model for state-owned companies and in order to implement an initiative even close to resembling the TVA it was necessary to overcome a further obstacle posed by the model for state-owned companies already addressed by legislation and deeply-rooted in practice.

The model for modern state-owned companies began in Italy with the creation of the Istituto di Riconversione Industriale (IRI) [Institute for Industrial Reconversion]. The founding of the IRI dates back to 1933, in the context of the great crisis and it is certainly no coincidence that its timing coincided with the creation of the TVA. The IRI was initially created as a temporary solution to manage banks' investments in industries taken over by the state to avoid a collapse of the banking system[195]. Already in 1937, the IRI was made a permanent institution, marking the beginning of the development of a system of companies in which the state has a controlling interest, following an original formula.

The IRI was called-upon to respect three fundamental rules. This institution was to pursue objectives established by the state; the IRI's strategy was to be aimed at serving the general interest, to be correctly historicised by government authorities. Companies linked to IRI were to maintain their juridical status of joint-stock companies (Inc.) and thus be regulated by private law. Finally, the IRI was obliged to respect market rules, not resorting to its privileged position deriving from its public status to distort competition in its own favour[196].

This original set-up was not always fully implemented in reality. According to this model, a state-owned company's task is to fill the voids left by private companies, whenever these appear inadequate for implementing initiatives needed for the country's development and modernisation. It is clear how such as role gave the IRI contractual power that was all the greater in proportion to the weakness of the economy's private element. It was the weakness of the Italian economy that was the cause of an involution of state-owned companies to increasingly lower levels of competitiveness.

---

195 Grassini, F.A., Scognamiglio, C. (eds) , *Stato e industria in Europa: l'Italia*, Il Mulino, Bologna, 1979.

196 Maraffi, M., *Politica ed economia in Italia: la vicenda dell'impresa pubblica degli anni '30 e degli anni '50*, Il Mulino, Bologna, 1999.

In the United States, state intervention in the economy began, with Theodore Roosevelt, in order to curb great concentrations of power such as those of a monopolistic nature. In the decades that followed, state intervention remained qualified by the objective of protecting the markets' balance, which could be distorted only by private groups. The state's involvement in the economy was never in a condition that allowed it to assume a privileged position, to the extent of compromising the private element. Consequently, the federal initiative did not address this non-existent risk.

The Italian case was a different one. State intervention was on numerous occasions requested by private companies experiencing a crisis. State-owned companies fill the void left by private ones as a direct consequence of their weakness. In various periods, Italian economic history has experienced a return of structural problems caused by a relative lack of capital and entrepreneurial capabilities[197]. These local conditions compromised the first initiatives assigned to the IRI, *de facto* relaxing the good governance obligation.

The turning point was marked by a decision made in 1956 to create an *ad hoc* ministry to govern state intervention in the economy. This decision marked the end of a period of gradual transformation that had begun due to the influence of the needs of a wartime economy and progressively developed in the course of the war and during the years of reconstruction that followed it. The creation of the a ministry for companies in which the state has a controlling interest, the *Ministero delle Partecipazioni Statali*, sanctioned the pre-eminence of the political governance of companies in which the state had a controlling interest, overcoming restrictions imposed by charters aimed at good governance es-

197 Saraceno, P., *Iniziativa privata e azione pubblica nei piani di sviluppo economico*, Giuffrè, Milan, 1959; Caselli, L., *L'impresa pubblica nell'economia di mercato*, Giuffrè, Milan, 1970.

tablished when the IRI was founded[198]. Entrepreneurial autonomy was therefore reduced and with it the objective of reconciling the two objectives of serving the general interest and respecting the markets' rules for companies in which the state had a controlling interest.

The model for Italian state-owned companies, initially closer to the successful model provided in the United States by the TVA, increasingly distanced itself from this to the detriment of its capability to achieve adequate levels of efficiency, costs and effectiveness, to ensure the competitiveness of its initiatives[199].

This distance from America's New Deal experience emerged with greater clarity when the country addressed the problem of the industrialization of the south[200].

The *Cassa del Mezzogiorno* was created in 1950 as an autonomous state-owned authority, with competences ranging from planning to implementation. Industrial development emerged as the key objective and one that was also hard to implement[201]. The International Bank of Reconstruction and Development (BIRS), and in particular Rosenstein-Rodan, participated in defining this project.

The two perspectives, on one hand that of the American economist and of the other that of the Italian authorities, emerged with extreme clarity on that occasion.

Rosenstein-Rodan saw the *Cassa del Mezzogiorno* as a means for strengthening southern Italy's economic-industrial system, in an international perspective and within the framework of an open economy. The Italian authorities considered it impossible to expose the south's bud-

---

198 Saraceno, P., "L'industrializzazione italiana: un processo che non ha precedenti nell'esperienza del mondo occidentale", in *Economia e Politica Industriale*, 8/88.

199 Usai, G., *L'efficienza nelle organizzazioni*, UTET, Turin, 2000; Usai, G., *Le organizzazioni nella complessità*, CEDAM, Padova, 2002.

200 Posner, M., Woolf, G., *Italian Public Enterprises*, Longman, London, 1967; Cianci, E., *La nascita dello Stato imprenditore*, Mursia, Milan, 1977.

201 Barucci, P., *Ricostruzione, pianificazione, mezzogiorno. La politica economica in Italia dal 1943 al 1955*, Il Mulino, Bologna, 1978.

ding industries to international competition from the very beginning, and opted for solutions that were ultimately protectionist or quasi-protectionist.

Consistently with his neo-liberalist ideas, formed in the course of the New Deal, Rosenstein-Rodan was in favour of the *Cassa del Mezzogiorno* having a charter guaranteeing it assumed a sense of responsibility. The Italian authorities considered placing the *Cassa del Mezzogiorno* under government protection a non-negotiable condition[202].

Between these two alternatives, that of the Italian authorities prevailed. This choice was to have extremely serious consequences in the years that followed. The *Cassa del Mezzogiorno* and the IRI would be burdened by economic management that was so inadequate it would lead both to liquidation. Northern Italy opened to the European market and experienced a process of intense development and modernisation, while southern Italy remained a prisoner of localisms obstructing the overcoming of historical backwardness[203].

This north-south dualism remains, thwarting at least some of the efforts made to overcome it.

In order to understand the conflict between these two perspectives, with all the implications involved, the moment at which the name for this institution was chosen is of emblematic importance.

With his personal experience of the successes achieved during the New Deal, Rosenstein-Rodan was in favour of creating an Authority, both in name and juridical-economic status, for the development of Southern Italy[204]. The name *Cassa del Mezzogiorno* was instead proposed by a great Italian public servant on the basis of one considera-

---

202 Rosenstein-Rodan, P.N., *Programming in Theory and Italian Practice*, MIT, Boston, 1955.

203 D'Antone, L. (edited by), *Radici storiche ed esperienza dell'intervento straordinario nel Mezzogiorno*, Bibliopolis, Napoli, 1996; Boccia, F., Leonardi, R., Letta, E., Treu, T., *I Mezzogiorni d'Europa*, Il Mulino, Bologna, 2003.

204 Rosenstein-Rodan, P.N., *The Objective of United States Economic Assistance Programs*, MIT, Boston, 1957.

tion: the word Authority was extraneous to the Italian lexicon while the word *"cassa"* instantly brought to mind the idea of resources available for financing development.

This contrast is reported here because it clearly expresses two different ideas of the state and of business. As previously mentioned, the TVA was created by the United States' federal government with an obligation to respect business good governance principles. This position is set within the framework of the idea of good governance *tout-court* which is part of the American tradition and originates in the Calvinist values of the country's Founding Fathers[205 206].

The *Cassa del Mezzogiorno* was instead set within a more complex idea of a state, the result of unification between regional states with different cultures and values. The person who came up with the name *Cassa del Mezzogiorno* can realistically be thought to have referred to the fact that southern regions, governed by the Bourbon state and by the Vatican State, would not easily have accepted managerial principles inspired by Calvinist traditions[207].

The Italian version of the New Deal was therefore achieved assigning a dual role to the state, that of entrepreneurship and that of providing subsidies. The *Cassa del Mezzogiorno*, adopting this duality developed on a basis that was undermined from the very beginning. The progressive prevalence of the subsidizing state over the entrepreneurial state inevitably led to the bankruptcy of the *Cassa del Mezzo-*

---

205 Guatri, L, Vicari, S., *Sistema d'impresa e capitalismi a confronto*, EGEA, Milan, 1994.

206 The topicality of this subject is at the centre of an analysis by Grassini, F., *L'indipendenza delle autorità*, Il Mulino, Bologna, 2001.

207 This alternative, albeit in new terms, re-emerged recently in the form of a concept. See Napolitano, S., Zoppini, A., *Le autorità al tempo della crisi. Per una riforma della regolazione e della vigilanza dei mercati*, Il Mulino, Bologna, 2009.

giorno and, more in general, that of the system involving companies in which the state had a controlling interest [208].

3.10 Financing development: instruments and rules

Many lessons are to be learned from the collapse of the *Cassa per il Mezzogiorno*. This experience, revisited briefly in previous pages, proves the predominant importance of rules compared to instruments for achieving good governance.

This issue is of the greatest importance for defining the amount of debt that institutions in the European Union are permitted to incur in, on the basis of order founded on subsidiarity.

The problem has two interrelated aspects.

The first consists in the amount of debt permitted. Establishing limits is necessary to avoid an institution draining resources to the disadvantage of others, since there is a limit established for resources available in financial markets.

The second aspect is the manner in which resources made available in this manner are used. The reason for this second aspect, is the fear that one institution's bad governance could affect others. This is all the more important when bad governance of resources results in an inability to honour debt servicing.

Resorting to an independent authority can be a means for simultaneously addressing both aspects of the aforementioned problem and it is in this sense that the experience acquired, starting precisely with the very prototype for such a solution, the creation of the TVA within the framework of the American New Deal, assumes importance.

---

208 Donati, D., Paci, A. (edited by), *Sussidiarietà e concorrenza. Una nuova prospettiva per la gestione dei beni comuni*, Il Mulino, Bologna, 2010.

The Italian case involving the *Cassa del Mezzogiorno* proves instead that resorting to an independent institution is not per se sufficient for guaranteeing the achievement of these same objectives. The TVA and the *Cassa del Mezzogiorno* were basically equivalent juridical instruments; the economic objectives pursued were also basically equivalent. Their diversity was in the rules that would lead their different fates.

The comparison proposed in previous pages between the TVA and the *Cassa del Mezzogiorno* has an emblematic value. It is important for identifying an interpretative criteria that can be applied to the state institution system as a whole.

Resorting to independent authorities, defined on the basis of the context in which they are situated, can be an instrument for guaranteeing state intervention or those of public interest on condition the rules of good governance are respected.

Establishing rules capable of guaranteeing the good governance of resources has a more general value, to the extent that these rules can be applied not only to independent authorities, but also to all the European Union's institutions.

The starting point in defining good governance rules for all the European Union institutions could be the contraposition between consumption and investment. Resorting to debt can be restricted to financing investments capable of generating revenue adequate for servicing the debt contracted.

Identifying a starting point for defining a new social-economic order is relevant since it can influence the point of arrival, the definition of which is the result of multiple factors. The context within which this process developed is equally important and in this book the context identified is that of a European social market economy.

It is the opinion of the author that it is correct to propose a method for addressing this problem and that is the meaning of the remarks above.

It would be an abstract exercise to set out a complete model, that cannot derive from theoretical reflections but must be the result of historicizing. It is ultimately society that shapes itself, through a historical process in which freedom to choose can be achieved following different paths.

Chapter IV. The Atlantic dimension of a social market economy

4.1 Centralization *versus* subsidiarity. A necessary convergence between the United States and the European Union

The American and European models of statehood present many points of contact as well as many important divergences, and the same applies to the two systems' social-economic models.

Relations between forms of neo-liberalism that emerged in the United States following the New Deal and corresponding tendencies that took root in core-Europe in the form of a social market economy have already been addressed in previous pages.

The analysis outlined in the third chapter of this book poses an extremely important question: whether or not a convergence between the United States and the European Union is feasible as far as good governance rules are concerned, and more specifically the regulating of state expenditure and limitations to sovereign debt[209].

A comparison between the organisation of sovereign debt in the United States and in Europe clearly reveals differences that are constantly undergoing further change. In the United States, sovereign debt is concentrated at a federal level, while in Europe, the Europe Commission does not have the right to resort to debt.

In Europe sovereign debt is held at a national and sub-national level, while states belonging to the Unites States federation resort to debt far less.

---

209 Glossner, C.L., Gregosz, D. (eds), *60 Years of Social Market Economy, Formation, Development and Perspectives of a Peacemaking Formula*, Konrad Adenauer Stiftung, Berlin, 2010.

This different distribution of debt, at the various levels in which the two federations are organised, is anything but neutral. In the United States debt is linked to a rising centralization of power, directly linked to the international economic and political role played by the country. In Europe, restrictions to the spending capabilities of European authorities allow the protection of constitutional order founded on the principle of subsidiarity, acknowledging ample autonomy to all national and local institutions[210].

These differences are also present in the characteristics assumed by the United States and European central banks.

The Federal Reserve System, originally endowed with ample authority, has become increasingly conditioned over time by federal authorities in Washington. The central bank's objective of protecting the value of currency and containing inflationary processes has gradually been replaced by the objective of financing federal expenditure, covering rising deficits by printing money and buying government bonds. This evolution has become easier to manage to the extent that the role played by the American dollar as a reserve currency, and one used globally for payments, has allowed the dollar and U.S. treasury bonds to be sold internationally[211].

The European system of central banks has been endowed with great autonomy; its activities have been obliged to respect orthodox monetary criteria to protect the value of the currency. This characteristic has remained in place and the ban on financing state authorities has played a decisive role in ensuring this. This monetary order is an essential element in European constitutional order, characterised by the rejection of high levels of centralization and the assertion of innovative

---

210 AA.VV., *Luigi Einaudi: istituzioni mercato e riforma sociale*, Accademia Nazionale dei Lincei, Rome, 2005.

211 Atkinson, A.B., Stiglitz, J.E., *Lectures on Public Economics*, McGraw-Hill, London, 1980.

forms of subsidiarity. The social aspects are equally important since inflation is a tax that affects those with less contractual power.

The charter of the European Central Bank is founded on an economic culture fuelled by liberal and Christian traditions that in Europe resulted in the principles of a social market economy.

In terms of centralisation and social imbalances, inflation has a dual impact. By inflationist money printing, a central bank can drain resources from the system, transferring control to central authorities. Inflation simultaneously transfers resources from those elements of society having less contractual power to those with more who are able to use the loss of currency value to their own advantage.

The ECB's charter was drafted so as to restrict these phenomena as much as possible. The difference between the American order, centralistic and characterized by the central bank depending on the federal administration, and the European order, which is subsidiary and characterised by the central bank's autonomy, is now at the centre of a wide-ranging debate. On one hand, in Europe some are in favour of reducing the European Central Bank's autonomy, rendering it more similar to the model provided by the Unites States, while, on the other hand, in the United States some are in favour of returning to the original order characterized by greater autonomy of the American central bank. These trends are clearly of constitutional importance and it would be reductive to discuss them in exclusively economic terms[212].

These apparently different positions of criticism, currently being expressed on both continents, in fact share the search for bringing closer together these two models of statehood, with all the consequent economic and social implications this involves. This can be interpreted as a symptom of an awareness of the need for the two systems to converge, in order to create a broad integrated area and one oriented, over the long term, towards increasing levels of unification. This interpreta-

212 A whimsical approach is developed by Savinio, A., *Scritti dispersi*, Adelphi, Milan, 2004.

tion envisages the possibility that the aforementioned critical positions are simply the more or less conscious expression of basic trends of historical importance. Ideas lead processes but can also be the result of the processes themselves[213].

By schematizing to the highest degree this analysis, it is possible to identify three alternative solutions towards which these systems may become oriented.

A first solution consists of changing the European model in terms of centralisation, bringing it closer to the current American order. This option includes positions in favour of issuing Eurobonds and of changing the ECB's charter, allowing it to become a lender of last resort with no restrictions imposed on amounts lent.

A second solution consists of changing the model in force in the United States, reiterating the central bank's autonomy and having as a priority the defence of the currency's value. This option includes positions in favour of establishing binding restrictions on state expenditure and supporting a reduction of centralisation.

A third solution could be described as an evolutionary compromise, capable of immediately supporting the convergence between the two systems, paving the way for a later definition of a shared economic-institutional order able to orient and support an Atlantic integration process[214].

One fundamental aspect in assessing these alternatives and their greater or lesser chances of being implemented, consists of the social implications involved.

---

213 This is a philosophical debate, fuelled during the 20th Century by Marxist interpretations, and one that goes beyond the specific object of this analysis. This point should be seen in this perspective and will be addressed on another occasion. On methodology see Caffè, F., *Economia del benessere*, Comunità, Milan, 1956.

214 Glossner, C.L., Gregosz, D., *The Formation and Implementation of the Social Market Economy by Alfred Müller-Armack and Ludwig Erhard*, Konrad Adenauer Stiftung, Berlin, 2011.

A Calvinist culture, deeply-rooted in the history of the United States, would certainly side with a centralised vision of the state and social order not necessarily based in solidarity.

The liberal-Christian culture, as a social market economy could be described, which characterises the European experience and *in primis* that of core-Europe, is certainly suited to a subsidiary order of statehood and social order based on solidarity.

Freedom is the value shared by these two perspectives, but is certainly susceptible to being presented in different ways.[215].

4.2 The evolution of United States statehood: from federalism to centralism to neo-federalism

Convergence between the United States and Europe can by fuelled by knowledge of the historical experience shared by these two continents. Both experienced phases of centralisation and decentralised development. This alternation of historical moments is more easily identifiable when referred to Europe, a continent that has experienced moments of radicalisation in some of its countries. This alternation can also be seen in American history, although this country has never experienced extreme events in the centralistic sense. Before independence, the United States was subjected to a centralistic government created by British colonialism. The United States Federal Constitution was written after independence by a political class formed by the War of Independence. Federate American states establish a constitutional order

215 Glossner, C.L., Gregosz, D. (eds), *60 Years of Social Market Economy*, op. cit.

that would prevent the government in Washington from replicating the centralisation of power suffered in the colonial era[216].

Experiencing two different forms of statehood could now allow these two federations to search for shared solutions drawing on their own heritage of experiences.

The United States' experience deserves greater attention since it has traditionally been analysed as the implementation of the federal model, while centralisation processes have not been the subject of a careful analysis. This, *in primis*, because the United States is the first great historical example of a federation and it is totally understandable that historical, juridical-economic and political analyses have privileged this aspect.

The American constitution has always been a reference point when an integration process between states has addressed the problem of organising a federal form of government or governance[217].

During the 19th Century, and even more so in the 20th century, the United States constitution evolved profoundly both at a formal and material level. Within the framework of the brief analysis carried out here, the most important aspect is to verify whether this process of change can be identified with breaking points, or significant change, providing lessons to better understand the current problems in relations between Europe and the United States[218].

One fundamental change, already addressed in previous pages, can be linked to the action implemented first by Theodore Roosevelt, and later by Franklin D. Roosevelt, to affirm a new balance between the state and the market, renewing the federal administration's initiatives. This change resulted in the New Deal during the Thirties.

---

216 In this sense one should bear in mind that the spark that started the War of Independence was a new tax imposed by Great Britain.

217 Spinelli, A., *Come ho tentato di diventare saggio*, op. cit.

218 This approach was developed over the years by Altiero Spinelli; see the many notes contained in his diaries published in three books by Paolini, E. (edited by), *Altiero Spinelli, Diario europeo*, Il Mulino, Bologna, 1989-1992.

The New Deal is traditionally seen as the answer to the Great Depression and in this manner attention is concentrated on its social-economic aspects.

The constitutional aspects are equally important, and all the more so for this analysis. The New Deal impressed an acceleration on the centralisation of power at the level of federal institutions[219]. This centralisation at the time reached relatively contained levels. Fiscal resources available to federal authorities were limited, the possibility to incur debt was very low, the federal central bank was bound to develop an orthodox monetary policy. Contact points with the all that the European Union is currently experiencing are obvious.

A second turning point, and a more radical one, began with World War II, when the United States assumed a central role in the world's political-economic order.

The role played by the American currency as a reserve currency and the one used for international payments allowed more money to be printed and federal bonds to be issued, which were easily placed both at home and increasingly more abroad. In this manner the United States federal government could centralise control over rising resources, draining resources from both the federate states and the international community.

The United States' federal organisation progressively evolved towards one increasingly characterised in national terms, losing key aspects of its original constitutional order. It is by definition an abstract to create a border between the two levels of centralisation. In the United States the centralising process that started in the Thirties experienced periods of acceleration linked above all to international events that resulted in increased expenditure. This process was an ongoing one and hence it would be arbitrary to rigidly compare a cen-

---

219 Leuchtenburg, W.E., *F.D. Roosevelt and the New Deal*, Harper&Row, New York, 1963.

tralisation with evolutionary characteristics, such as the New Deal, to excessive centralisation with an involutional impact.

The year 1971, when the crisis experienced by the dollar determined the end of the monetary order founded in Bretton Woods, could be symbolically used as a border. This schematisation can be used for interpretative means, to provide order to a series of phenomena, not to be used as criteria for assessment applicable in an a-critical way.

There are many phenomena that can be assessed using this interpretative schematisation. At an institutional level this orientation allows one to understand the changing of the role played by the Federal Reserve, which had become the federal government's instrument for economic-monetary policy, with decreasing levels of autonomy. At a social-economic level, this orientation allows one to understand some of the basic reasons for the debate that developed in the United States favouring the rule imposing a balanced budget in order to bind federal expenditure and reduce the centralising process. Similar considerations can be applied to movements in favour of a return to the original federal order which have more recently appeared in the United States. Many other phenomena can also be assessed in this manner.

It is possible to retrieve the three alternatives set out in the first paragraph of this chapter and provide them with a specific interpretation within the framework of relations between the United States and the European Union. These three alternatives could then be rewritten, with unchanged logic, in the following manner, also so as to understand the risks and potential of the transition phase currently experienced by the European Union and the United States.

The future could correspond to one of these scenarios or follow intermediate solutions. What is important for this analysis is to understand the alternatives taking shape as well as their implications, in order to understand the emerging phenomena that consolidated interpretative criteria are incapable of fully assessing.

A first scenario is the reaffirmation at an Atlantic level, with renewed modalities, of the New Deal experience. Europe is renovating its state-market relations, just as the New Deal did. In the absence of serious international responsibilities, the level of centralisation that Europe may equip itself with repeating the American experience of the 1930s could be stabilised, taking into account adaptations made necessary firstly by the passing of time. The rising level of centralisation experienced by the United States during the decades that followed the New Deal may not reappear in the European case. The variable on which the possibility that this should take place mostly depends, at an international level, is the organisation or not of a large defensive apparatus. At an internal level, the most sensitive variable is European economic-industrial policy. The most recent European experience proves that it is possible to develop innovative policies privileging a capacity to direct, as an alternative to the direct management and centralised funding of projects. The "Europe of Projects"[220] differs greatly from more recent American industrial policy, which has been implemented in strategic sectors as an element of defence expenditure. Unlike the American experience, in the European case it is ultimately difficult to envisage a centralisation of social expenditure to make up for national deficiencies; most European countries have traditionally developed advanced forms of social policy.

Should Europe embark upon this path and if the United States should question the level of centralisation developed since the end of World War II, then a basically homogeneous picture will emerge at an Atlantic level[221].

---

220 Velo, D., (a cura di), *L'Europe dei progetti*, op. cit.

221 Orientations and options chosen in the course of the New Deal can be revisited and compared to the current context. The topicality of the debate at the time will impress scholars. Romasco, A.U., *Roosevelt's New Deal. The Politics of Recovery*, op. cit.

A reduction of the level of centralisation in the United States implies a reduction in policies addressed at international leadership, in order to reorient resources towards internal objectives. The correlation between the two aspects of the country's strategic repositioning are ostensibly inseparable; experience accumulated since the end of World War II confirms this correlation.

This scenario has points of contact with the experience matured by the United States before the Second World War, but does not coincide with it. History does not precisely repeat the experiences of the past, but can only relive them on condition they are profoundly transformed. After experiencing centralisation, it is unrealistic to envisage a return to traditional forms of federalism as defined by Founding Fathers Hamilton, Jay and Madison, while there may instead be the prospect of new forms of neo-federalism, in synergy with innovative forms of statehood such as the European Union could be described.

This scenario could be characterised by decreasing centralisation, by the creation of new forms of welfare, by widespread subsidiarity. It is possible to identify a number of basic tendencies without setting out solutions that will be gradually historicised in the course of the process. In this context, cooperation between the United States and the European Union is destined to be of fundamental strategic importance.

A second possible scenario depends firstly on the different options chosen by the United States, in the sense of confirming the progressive centralisation process. A choice made in this sense could result in the disintegration of a series of international relations. Such a scenario consists of the possibility that the United States' energy be concentrated on defending its international role, to the disadvantage of internal social-economic objectives. There is a historical precedent that can clarify the more important implications of such a choice. Faced with fundamental choices regarding its international role, in the first half of the 20th Century, Great Britain made choices privileging the former instead of other objectives, ultimately making choices that correspond to the second scenario envisaged for the United States in current conditions[222]. History tells us what the internal and international consequences of these choices have been for Great Britain. This precedent is helpful for understanding, with a non-deterministic approach, a number of tendencies that could be repeated, certainly not entirely corresponding, should the United States opt for the choices outlined in the second scenario.

A third scenario could be an alternative to the two radical options described above, bearing in mind the remarks made in the first paragraph of this chapter. This scenario would present aspects of continuity with the current situation while simultaneously be characterised by an attempt to comply with the requirements underlying the two aforementioned scenarios. This third scenario, which could be merged with the first or the second alternative, can be seen as a form of transition from the old order to a new one.

It is clear that possible alternative scenarios could be implemented, not only depending on decisions assumed independently by the United States. They must inevitably address changes in the international order that will arise due to initiatives taken by the European Union and new emerging countries.

---

222 Velo, D., *La crisi economica internazionale e l'alternativa europea*, op. cit.

4.3 A historical precedent

The United States and Europe had already experienced innovative forms of Atlantic cooperation before the end of World War II with what after the war became globally known as the Marshall Plan, or the European Recovery Program (ERP)[223].

It is in the genesis of this initiative and the impulse provided by the Roosevelt administration to its implementation, that one discovers the mark of the thesis presented by Jean Monnet, involved not only in material reconstruction, but above all in the institutional reconstruction of a new Europe.

The Marshall Plan, implemented after 1945, marked a turning point in the United States' strategy for the reconstruction of Europe. It was also the bearer of a project for constitutional order addressed at bringing Europe and the United States closer. The objective was to have interlocutors on both sides of the ocean who would be capable of cooperating in implementing a shared project, based on values and long-term objectives. Having all European countries achieve a continental federal dimension seemed to be an indefeasible requirement to ensure the equality of Europe and the United States, firstly as far as size was concerned. The continental aspect was essential for overcoming national or nationalist perspectives and for planning an Atlantic convergence.

If this interpretation is correct, the United States assumed responsibility for orienting European countries to move beyond the national dimension when making economic and political choices. It is legitimate to also envisage that this far-sighted plan also contained an awareness of how difficult it would be in the decades to come for

223 Hogan, M.J., "European Integration and the Marshall Plan", in *The Marshall Plan: a Retrospective*, edited by Stanley Hoffman and Charles Maier, Boulder 1984.

America to maintain international leadership, in the absence of a well-qualified partnership in a regime of shared sovereignty with a united Europe. Over the short term, a united and democratic Europe was essential to the United States as a guarantee of greater political stability throughout western Europe. The civil and democratic reconstruction of European states was functional to the implementation of this plan, and also necessary.

Since the end of World War II, for the first time one observed international policies moving from strategy based on intervention and the creation of bilateral relations between countries, to a strategy of cooperation between one country, the United States, and an integration process between a number of countries, the European nations. This change was all the more important since the United States has supported the European integration process[224].

This process considered the creation of a supra-national institution as a necessary requirement. In other words, it was necessary to create an interlocutor capable of establishing a dialogue with the United States in the name of all European countries. On April 16th 1948 the Organization for European Economic Cooperation (OEEC) was founded; it was the embryo of the model for Atlantic cooperation. Within the OEEC discussions began on issues such as cooperation, the reduction of trade barriers, the creation of single European customs, the stabilisation of currencies and shared labour policies[225].

The new scenario that in those years opened to Europe, and the opportunities created for nations joining the process, supported the development of shared and long-term supranational strategies.

---

224 The history of European integration and the steps that were to follow beginning with Schuman's statement in 1950 and initiatives taken by Jean Monnet, are not the object of this analysis. On this subject and for a more in-depth analysis of the Marshall Plan, see Velo, F., "I Piani europei e la ricostruzione delle città italiane nel secondo dopoguerra. Sviluppo sociale, economico, industriale", op. cit.

225 See Spierenburg, D., Poidevin, R., *The History of the High Authority of the European Coal and Steel Community*, Weinfeld and Nicolson, London 1994.

The American contribution to the beginning of the European integration process was essential at this stage and was manifested in many ways.

Aid to Europe, started during the war for single allied countries and continued after the war within the framework of the Marshall Plan, was a fundamental part of this strategy.

Such aid was conditioned by the United States to its being managed in a unified manner by European countries.

The same applies to monetary aspects. To support the European currencies' return to convertibility, the United States supported the creation of a monetary union, capable of orienting the intervention of central banks and the European states' economic authorities towards shared solutions.

A similar interpretation can be used to analyse American intervention in the German constituent process that would result in the approval of a constitution with federal characteristics, organised on the basis of the American constitutional model.

In summary, it is possible to perceive how after 1943 and above all immediately after the war, the United States intervened with a decisive impact in European economic-political reorganisation, specifically influencing constituent processes, orienting them towards united European solutions and the incorporation of federal solutions[226].

Influence at the time was unidirectional. The United States oriented Europe towards a federal model, perceived as a prerequisite favourable to the development of balanced Atlantic cooperation.

This historical precedent emphasises how international cooperation can be extended to the more strictly constitutional dimension in innovative ways, radically modifying the forms and contents of traditional diplomacy.

226 These aspects have been broadly addressed in historical, economic and political literature. See Clayton, W. United States Secretary of State . Internal memorandum dated May 27th 1947.

In current conditions, this precedent poses a problem; that of how cooperation between Europe and the United States can assume a constitutional dimension, at what conditions and with which contents.

The author is convinced that under current conditions, cooperation of this importance can only realistically exist on condition it is perceived as bidirectional, hence as a process shared on the basis of an equal partnership. This point will be addressed in greater detail in the next pages.

4.4 The Gramm-Rudman-Hollings Act

A vast debate has been held in recent years in the United States, influenced by schools of thought more in favour of privileging internal social-economic development and of reducing federal expenditure and the level of centralisation, adapting the country's foreign policy to the changes that have come about in international equilibriums. This debate has been referred to in previous pages, perceiving how it confirms the possibility of closer relations between the United States and the European Union, both as far as a model of statehood is concerned – and *in primis* the level of centralisation – as well as the social-economic model. It is in this context that the points of contact historically established between New Deal neo-liberalism and the European social market economy assume importance.

In order to assess the importance of this debate, reference to the Gramm-Rudman-Hollings Act[227] plays an important role. In 1985 three senators decided to sponsor a draft bill called the Balanced Budget and Emergency Deficit Control Act addressed at reforming

227 P.L. 99-177, Approved December 12, 1985 (99 Stat. 1037).

American fiscal policy. This Act is nowadays commonly referred to using the names of the three senators who sponsored it.

The initiative's contingent motivation arose from concern created by the high deficit level that had characterised American fiscal policy in previous years, due to policies implemented by President Reagan. In this context this Act could have been perceived as the Senate's attempt to bring federal spending under control, stating the objective of balancing the federal budget through legislation. There were of course more important grounds for this decision, consisting of the aforementioned contingency projected over the long term, which was an attempt to re-establish a constitutional order that respected the autonomy of member states regards to federal institutions.

In this perspective, the Gramm-Rudman-Hollings Act could be seen as an attempt to reduce the centralism that had developed due to the combined effects of internal and international policies. This tendency had experienced an acceleration in more recent years, blamed on the Republican administration in power, but had far older roots irrespective of whether Republicans or Democrats governed.

The draft bill followed repeated requests to approve rules of constitutional importance that would guarantee respect for real fiscal federalism, presented by a number of member states in previous years.

The Act presented one critical aspect that has been the reason for its lack of success[228]. It envisaged automatic mechanisms for cutting expenditure should federal parliamentary assemblies approve budget deficits over the limits established by this law. This provision was declared unconstitutional by the Supreme Court with a ruling passed in 1986 soon after the Act was approved.

Even in the absence of this ruling on unconstitutionality, it is legitimate to address the Balanced Budget and Emergency Deficit Control Act's real capacity to achieve the objectives pursued.

---

228 For a more in-depth analysis see Velo. F., "Fiscal Federalism: from the Gramm-Rudman-Hollings Act to the Atlantic Maastricht Treaty", op. cit.

The Act did not take into account two aspects; the country's international role, destined to influence internal equilibriums, and the dollar's international role, which allowed the United States to resort to international debt in order to finance federal expenditure.

This phenomenon was originally studied in many of its fundamental aspects by Robert Triffin and the so-called "Triffin dilemma" provides an interpretation of international monetary imbalances that is still valid today[229].

The logic followed by the three senators who sponsored this bill is an expression of the American tradition. A balanced budget is the rule for all member states and for all other institutions. The United States' privileged international position has exercised an influence that goes against such order. The possibility of orienting resources at an international level has weakened the rigour of public finance at all levels. The federal government has been unable to respect the balanced budget rule; the federal government's inclination to approve deficits has spread, albeit to a limited extent, also to other institutions.

The Gramm-Rudman-Hollings Act could be compared to the Maastricht Treaty. As far as objectives are concerned, there is a broad convergence between the American Act and the European treaty. In both cases the objective is to impose respect for the obligation to present a balanced budget as the basis for federal fiscal order[230].

The Maastricht Treaty assumed as reference parameters for deficits and permitted indebtedness, the ones that at the time were applied also by the United States. It was only later that a slight gap appeared. This is an aspect of crucial importance in assessing the possibility of closer relations and integration between the economies on the two shores of the Atlantic.

---

229 Triffin, R., *Gold and the Dollar Crisis*, op. cit.

230 Maillet, P., "L'Europe comme réponse aux défis du XXI siècle", in *The European Union Review*, 1/02.

4.5 The Atlantic social market economy

The conclusions reached in the previous paragraph suggest that the Maastricht Treaty and a United States provision inspired by the Gramm-Rudman-Hollings Act could be developed along parallel lines, one strengthened by the other, creating the basis for shared fiscal rules on which increasingly closer integration between the two Atlantic federations could be founded. This hypothesis involves the tendency of the dollar and the euro to assume an increasingly homogeneous role, to the extent of establishing fixed exchange rates between the two currencies. This hypothesis would also involve profound changes in the policies implemented by the two federations in the economic and social sectors[231].

This idea has its roots in the fact that both the United States and Europe are now facing problems what would be more easily overcome on the basis of a shared strategy, since the nature of the issues the two systems are called upon to address is a common one.

There is one point that is of the utmost importance for explaining the significance of this possible convergence.

Although starting from different points, the United States and Europe are now united by the fact that they are called upon to change their development model, based on budget deficits and debt. Experience proves how difficult it is to obtain consensus for change within the country where there are possible alternatives. As Machiavelli has taught us, new order finds unenthusiastic defenders among those who may benefit from change, while it finds proud enemies among those who benefitted from the old order. This applies all the more to change that demands current sacrifices in view of future advantages.

231 Hutton, W., *Europa vs Usa*, ed. it. Fazi, Rome, 2003; Wallace, H., Wallace, W., (eds), *Policy making in the European Union*, Oxford University Press, Oxford, 2000.

The objective of a balanced budget and the reduction of public debt accumulated by all the European and American institutions, on which a renewed form of fiscal federalism could be founded, is more difficult to achieve on the basis of an autonomous European project and an autonomous one implemented by the United States. An Atlantic agreement reached in this sense would allow both federations to proceed more easily in this direction.

The history of the European integration process shows that all progress has coincided with a period of crisis that questioned everything achieved so far[232]. This lesson could encourage a search for shared solutions at an Atlantic level in order to address the crisis shared by both systems.

The problem to be address consists of the need to change the two federation's internal order as well as simultaneously and in synergy changing international order.

As always, the greatest problem consists in identifying the crucial problems to be addressed, as a condition for starting a process. The search for solutions is easier, since it is of a technical nature. The identification of problems addresses broader issues, since it questions the historical aspects of processes that may be activated.

It is an essential opinion of the author that both the federations overlooking the Atlantic are today called upon to question their development models, providing answers to society's increasingly pressing demands. What is up for debate includes relations between the economy and society, relations between society and the state, the division of roles between the state and the market, welfare reform, sustainable development and the need to reorganise productive processes so they respect the environment. This is not a complete list. It is, however, sufficient for understanding the extent of possible transformations.

232 Albertini, M., *Una rivoluzione pacifica. Dalle Nazioni all'Europa*, Il Mulino, Bologna, 1999.

These transformations question social order as well as relations between the state, the market and society, relations between central power and local authorities and international order.

In this context the crucial issue is therefore whether a social market economy can become a shared objective for the European Union and the United States in order to integrate these two societies while acknowledging their differences.

This new order must be capable of combining freedom, solidarity and new forms of democratic participation in a manner that is coherent with forces emerging in the 21st century.

Should such a project turn out to be feasible for the United States and the European Union following a gradual convergence, it could spread at an international level as an alternative to the anarchic liberism that has marked the end of the 20th Century.

References

AA.VV., "The evolution of economic governance in EMU", *Economic Papers* n. 328, European Commission, Brussels, 2008.

AA.VV., *La cooperazione rafforzata e l'Unione Economica*, Giuffrè, Milan, 2007.

AA.VV., *An Agenda for a Growing Europe*, Oxford University Press, Oxford, 2004.

AA.VV., *Luigi Einaudi: istituzioni mercato e riforma sociale*, Accademia Nazionale dei Lincei, Rome, 2005.

Aaron, R., Lerner, D., *La querelle de la CED*, Plon, Paris, 1956.

Albertini, M., *Il federalismo*, Il Mulino, Bologna, 1986.

Albertini, M., *Tutti gli scritti*, Il Mulino, Bologna, various years.

Albertini, M., *Una rivoluzione pacifica. Dalle Nazioni all'Europa*, Il Mulino, Bologna, 1999.

Artis, M., Nixon, F. (eds), *The Economics of the European Union*, Oxford University Press, Oxford, 2007.

Atkinson, A.B., Stiglitz, J.E., *Lectures on Public Economics*, McGraw-Hill, London, 1980.

Baimbridge, M. , Whyman, P. (eds), *Fiscal Federalism and European Economic Integration*, Routledge, London, 2004.

Barucci, P., *Ricostruzione, pianificazione, mezzogiorno. La politica economica in Italia dal 1943 al 1955*, Il Mulino, Bologna, 1978.

Baumann, Z., *Voglia di comunità*, ed. it. Laterza, Bari, 2011.

Beck, U., Giddens, A., Lash, S., *Modernizzazione riflessiva*, ed. it. Asterios, Trieste, 1999.

Becker, M., *La banque européenne d'investissement*, La Documentation Française, Paris, 1973.

Benedetti, A., *Certezza pubblica e "certezze" private*, Giuffrè, Milan, 2011.

Benevolo, L., *Storia dell'architettura moderna*, Laterza, Bari, 1960.

Bermejo, R., "La Banque Européenne d'investissement", in *Revue Internationale de Droit économique*, 1/88.

Bini Smaghi, L., Padoa-Schioppa, T., Papadia, F., "The Transition to EMU in the Maastricht Treaty", *Essays in international finance*, 194/94.

Boccia, F., Leonardi, R., Letta, E., Treu, T., *I Mezzogiorni d'Europa*, Il Mulino, Bologna, 2003.

Boehm, F., Eucken, W., Grossmann-Doerth, H., *Ordnung der Wirtschaft*, Kohlhammer, Stuttgart, 1936.

Bognetti, G., *Lo spirito del costituzionalismo americano*, Giappichelli, Turin, 1998.

Bottinelli, L., Pavione, E., *Distretti industriali e cluster tecnologici: strategie emergenti di valorizzazione della ricerca e dell'innovazione*, Giuffrè, Milan, 2011.

Brumila, A., Buti, M., Franco, D., *The Stability and Growth Pact. The Architecture of Fiscal Policy in EMU*, Palgrave, London, 2001.

Bruzzi, S., "Impresa comune e perseguimento dell'interesse generale", in *Quaderno della rivista Servizi Pubblici e Appalti*, 2/06.

Bruzzi, S., *Impresa pubblica, sviluppo industriale e mezzogiorno: l'attualità della lezione di Pasquale Saraceno*, Jean Monnet Interregional Centre of Excellence, Pavia, 2011.

Buti, M., Franco, D., Pench, L.R. (eds), *The Welfare in Europe. Challenges and Reforms*, Edwar Elgar, Northampton, 1999.

Caffè, F., *Economia del benessere*, Comunità, Milan, 1956.

Caselli, L., *L'impresa pubblica nell'economia di mercato*, Giuffrè, Milan, 1970.

Castles, F.G., *The Future of the Welfare State. Crisis Myths and Crisis Realities*, Oxford University Press, Oxford, 2004.

Chandler, L.V., *America's Greatest Depression, 1929-1941*, Harper & Row, New York, 1970.

Cianci, E., *La nascita dello Stato imprenditore*, Mursia, Milan, 1977.

Commission for the Study of Economic and Monetary Union (Delors Report), *Report on Economic and Monetary Union in the European Community*, European Commission, Luxembourg, 1989.

Commission of the European Communities, *Communication from the Commission to the European Parliament, the Council, the European Economic and Social Committee and the Committee of the Regions. Cohesion Policy: Strategic Report 2010 on the Implementation of the Programmes 2007-2013*, Commission of the European Communities, Brussels, 2010.

Commission of the European Communities, Directorate-General Environment, *Policy News: Elena Supports Cities and Regions in Developing Sustainable Solutions*, Commission of the European Communities, Brussels, 2010.

Commission of the European Communities, *Jeremie: a Joint Regio-EIF-EIB Initiative Supporting Improved Access to Finance for EMSs*, Commission of the European Communities, Brussels, 2006.

Commission of the European Communities, *Jessica: Ioint European Support for Sustainable Investment in City Areas*, Commission of the European Communities, Brussels, 2006.

Constantinesco, V., Pierré-Caps, G., *Droit constitutionnel*, Paris, PUF, 2004.

Cordier, D., *J. Moulin*, Vol. I, II, III, Lattés, Paris, various years.

Croce, B., Einaudi, L., *Liberismo e liberalismo*, Ricciardi, Milan, 1957.

Croce, B., *Etica e politica*, Laterza, Bari, 1945.

D'Addio, M. (edited by), *Opere scelte di Luigi Sturzo. Stato, Parlamento e Partiti*, Laterza, Bari, 1992.

D'Antone, L. (edited by), *Radici storiche ed esperienza dell'intervento straordinario nel Mezzogiorno*, Bibliopolis, Napoli, 1996.

Directorate-General Mobility and Transport, *Mid-term Review of the 2007-2013 TEN-T Multi Annual Work Programme Project Portfolio*, Commission of the European Union, Brussels, 2010.

Donati, D., Paci, A. (edited by), *Sussidiarietà e concorrenza. Una nuova prospettiva per la gestione dei beni comuni*, Il Mulino, Bologna, 2010.

Eichengreen, B., *The European Economy since 1945. Coordinated Capitalism and Beyond*, Princeton University Press, Princeton, 2007.

Einaudi, L., *La guerra e l'unità europea*, Comunità, Milan, 1950.

Einaudi, L., "Il mio piano non è quello di Keynes", *La riforma sociale*, 2/33.

Einaudi, L., "Le premesse del ragionamento economico", *Rivista di Storia Economica*, 3/41.

Einaudi, L., *Il buongoverno*, Laterza, Bari, 1954.

Einaudi, L., *Le cause economiche della guerra*, Capolago, 1944.

Einaudi, L., *Lo scrittoio del Presidente*, Einaudi, Turin, 1956.

Einaudi, L., *Prediche inutili*, Einaudi, Torino, 1954.

Emerson, E., *La nuova economia europea*, ed. it. Il Mulino, Bologna, 1990.

Erhard, L., *Benessere per tutti*, ed. it. Garzanti, Milano, 1957.

Erhard, L., *La politica economia della Germania. Per un'economia sociale di mercato*, ed. it. Garzanti, Milan, 1962.

Eucken, W., *I fondamenti dell'economia politica*, ed. it. Sansoni, Florence, 1951.

European Commission, Directorate-General for Internal Policies, *The Implications of EIB and EBRD Co-financing for the EU Budget*, European Parliament, Brussels, 2011.

European Investment Bank, *The Loan Guarantee Instrument for Trans-European Transport Network Projects*, EIB, Luxembourg, 2008.

European Investment Fund, *Jeremie. Joint European Resources for Micro to Medium Enterprises Progress Report on Evaluation and Implementation Activities in 27 EU Member States*, European Investment Bank, Luxembourg, 2007.

Felice, F., *L'economia sociale di mercato*, Rubbettino, Soveria Mannelli, 2008.

Felice, F., *Luigi Sturzo e l'economia sociale di mercato*, C.I.S.S., Rome, 2011.

Felisini, D., *Inseparabili: lo Stato, il mercato e l'ombra di Colbert*, Rubbettino, Soveria Mannelli, 2010.

Felisini, D., Velo, D., "L'Unione Europea e la società europea", in AA.VV., *L'Unione Europea e la società europea*, Jean Monnet Interregional Centre of Excellence, Pavia, 2010.

Fenske, H., *Il pensiero politico contemporaneo*, ed. it. Il Mulino, Bologna, 2001.

Ferrari, F. (edited by), *Federalismo, sistema fiscale, autonomie. Modelli giuridici comparati*, Donzelli, Rome, 2010.

Fontana, G., *Le vie dell'industrializzazione europea: sistemi a confronto*, Il Mulino, Bologna, 1997.

Forte, F., Felice F. (eds), *Il liberalismo delle regole. Genesi ed eredità dell'economia sociale di mercato*, Rubbettino, Rome, 2010.

Forte, F., *Luigi Einaudi, il mercato e il buongoverno*, Einaudi, Turin, 1982.

Foster, H. (ed), *Postmodern Culture*, The Cromwell Press, Trowbridge, 1983.

Galgano, F., *Le istituzioni dell'economia di transizione*, Zanichelli, Bologna, 1978.

Gigliobianco, A. (edited by), *Luigi Einaudi: libertà, economia e coesione sociale*, Laterza, Bari, 2010.

Gilbert, P., Greppi, E., Marchegiani, G., Ratti, G., *La Banca Europea per gli Investimenti*, Pirola, Milan, 1991.

Glossner, C.L., Gregosz, D. (eds), *60 Years of Social Market Economy, Formation, Development and Perspectives of a Peacemaking Formula*, Konrad Adenauer Stiftung, Berlin, 2010.

Glossner, C.L., Gregosz, D., *The Formation and Implementation of the Social Market Economy by Alfred Müller-Armack and Ludwig Erhard*, Konrad Adenauer Stiftung, Berlin, 2011.

Goldschmidt, N., Wohlgemut, M., *Grundtexte zur friburger tradition der ordnung oekonomik*, Mohr, Tubingen, 2008.

Grassini, F.A., Scognamiglio, C. (eds), *Stato e industria in Europa: l'Italia*, Il Mulino, Bologna, 1979.

Grassini, F., *L'indipendenza delle autorità*, Il Mulino, Bologna, 2001.

Gros, D., Thygesen, N., *European monetary integration*, Longman, London, 1992.

Grosser, D., Lange, Th., Müller-Armack, A., Neuss, B., *Soziale marktwirtschaft-gescichte-konzept-leistung"*, Kohlhammer, Stuttgart, 1988.

Guatri, L, Vicari, S., *Sistema d'impresa e capitalismi a confronto*, EGEA, Milan, 1994.

Guccione, E. (edited by), *Luigi Sturzo e la democrazia nella prospettiva del terzo millennio*, Olschki, Florence 2004.

Habermas, J., *La crisi della razionalità nel capitalismo futuro*, ed. it. Laterza, Bari, 1975.

Habermas, J., *La costellazione postnazionale. Mercato globale, nazioni e democrazia*, ed. it Feltrinelli, Milano, 2002.

Hamilton, A., Madison, J., Jay, J., *The Federalist*, McLean, New York, 1788.

Harrop, J., *An Evaluation of the European Investment Bank: prospect and retrospect*, SUERF Series, 23/78.

Hasse, R.H., Schneider, H., Weigelt, K. (eds), *Social Market Economy. History, Principles and Implementation*, Schoening, Paderborn, 2008.

Hessel, S., *Indignez vous!*, Indigene, Montpellier, 2011.

Hirsch, E., *Ainsi va la vie*, Fondation Jean Monnet pour l'Europe, Lausanne, 1988.

Hogan, M.J., "European Integration and the Marshall Plan", in *The Marshall Plan: a Retrospective*, edited by Stanley Hoffman and Charles Maier, Boulder 1984.

Hutton, W., *Europa vs Usa*, ed. it. Fazi, Rome, 2003.

Izzo, L., "Presentazione", in AA.VV, *La Banca Europea per gli Investimenti*, Pirola, Milan, 1991.

Jozzo, A. (edited by), *The international monetary system and economic recovery*, Thema, Turin, 1979.

Jozzo, A., Velo, D., "L'autonomia della banca centrale in Italia e in Europa", in *Moneta e Credito*, 134/81.

Kindleberger, A.P., *The World in Depression, 1929-1939*, Allenlane, London, 1973.

Kuhn, T., *La struttura delle rivoluzioni scientifiche*, ed. it. Einaudi, Turin, 1968.

Lamfalussy, A., "Macro-coordination of fiscal policies in an Economic and Monetary Union in Europe", in AA.VV. *Report on Economic and Monetary Union in the European Community*, Office for official publications of the European Communities, Luxembourg, 1988.

Leuchtenburg, W.E., *F.D. Roosevelt and the New Deal*, Harper&Row, New York, 1963.

Lombardi Vallauri, L., *Corso di filosofia del diritto*, Milani, Padova, 1981.

Louis, J.V., *L'Union Européenne et sa monnaie*, ULB - Université Libre de Bruxelles, Brussels, 2009.

Louit, C., "Fédéralism fiscal: l'expérience française d'après Maastricht", *The European Union Review*, 3/97.

Luisi, J.V. (edited by), *Vers un système européen de banques centrales*, ULB - Université Libre de Bruxelles, Brussels, 1989.

Lyotard, J.F., *La condizione post-moderna*, ed. it. Feltrinelli, Milan, 1982.

Magnifico, G., *Euro: squilibri finanziari e spiragli di soluzione*, Luiss University Press, Rome, 2008.

Maillet, P., Velo D., *Europe à géometrie variable, transition vers l'intégration*, L'Harmattan, Paris, 1994.

Maillet, P., "Quelle organisation monétaire dans une Europe élargie a géométrie variable organisée?", *The European Union Review*, 1/96.

Maillet, P., "Un modéle de governance Européen favorable à l'apparition d'une politique diversifiée et cordonnée", *The European Union Review*, 1-2/01.

Maillet, P., "L'Europe comme réponse aux défis du XXI siècle", in *The European Union Review*, 1/02.

Majocchi, A., "Dallo EMS all'Economic Union e Monetaria: il ruolo della politica fiscale", *Il Federalista*, 1-2/80.

Majocchi, A., *Il coordinamento delle politiche nel nuovo modello di federalismo fiscale*, Pavia University, Pavia, 2004.

Majocchi, L.V., *La difficile costruzione dell'unità europea*, Jaca Book, Milan, 1996.

Maraffi, M., *Politica ed economia in Italia: la vicenda dell'impresa pubblica degli anni '30 e degli anni '50*, Il Mulino, Bologna, 1999.

Matarazzo, R. (edited by), *Democracy in the EU after the Lisbon Treaty*, Edizioni Nuova Cultura, Rome, 2011.

Melchionni, M.G., "Charles de Gaulle and Jean Monnet: two differing strategies for Europe", *The European Union Review*, 3/00.

Melchionni, M.G., *Altiero Spinelli et Jean Monnet*, Fondation Jean Monnet pour l'Europe, Lausanne, 1993.

Monnet, J., *Mémoires*, Fayard, Paris, 1976.

Montani, G., "The Government of the Economy in Europe. A post-Keynesian approach", in *The European Union Review*, 3/98.

Mosconi, F., "The Age of European Champions. A new Chance for EU Industrial Policy", in *The European Union Review*, 1/06.

Mosconi, F., *La Banque Européenne d'Investissement*, Centre de Recherches Européennes, Lausanne, 1977.

Müller-Armack, A., *Religion und wirtschaft geistes geschtiliche hinter guende unserer europaischen lebensform*, Kohlhammer, Stuttgart, 1959.

Müller-Graff, P.C., "Subsidiarity as a legal principle", *The European Union Review*, 1/96.

Müller-Graff, P.C., "The Treaty of Amsterdam. Characteristics and Perspectives", *The European Union Review*, 2/00.

Musgrave, R.M., *The Theory of Public Finance*, McGraw-Hill, New York, 1959.

Musil, R., *L'uomo senza qualità*, ed. it. Einaudi, Turin, 1962.

Napolitano, S., Zoppini, A., *Le autorità al tempo della crisi. Per una riforma della regolazione e della vigilanza dei mercati*, Il Mulino, Bologna, 2009.

Nardi, F., Pontolillo, V., Tresoldi, C., *Gli investimenti industriali ed il loro finanziamento tramite gli istituti di credito speciale*, Banca d'Italia, Rome, 1973.

Nicholls, A.J., *Freedom with responsibility. Social market economy in Germany 1918-1963*, Clarendon Press, Oxford, 1994.

North, D.C., *Istituzioni, cambiamento istituzionale e evoluzione dell'economia*, ed. it. Il Mulino, Bologna, 1994.

Padoa-Schioppa, T., *Il governo dell'economia*, Il Mulino, Bologna, 1997.

Padoa-Schioppa, T., *La lunga via per l'Euro*, Il Mulino, Bologna, 2004.

Palermo, F., *La forma di stato dell'Unione Europea*, CEDAM, Padova, 2005.

Palladino, G., *Don Sturzo oggi*, La Nuova Cultura Editrice, Naples, 1995.

Paolini, E. (edited by), *Altiero Spinelli, Diario europeo*, Il Mulino, Bologna, 1989-1992.

Paolini, E., *Altiero Spinelli. Appunti per una biografia*, Il Mulino, Bologna, 1988.

Papadia, F., "Unione Economica e Monetaria dopo Maastricht", *Il Mulino*, 339/92.

Papisca, A., "Europe 2020: what Compass, what Soul, which kind of Architecture for the EU Governance? The Need of Human Rights Mainstreaming", in *Peace Human Rights*, 3/10.

Papisca, A., "Barack Obama and Herman van Rompuy. New Leadership to educate international politics", *The European Union Review*, 1-2/11.

Peacock, A., Willgerondt, H. (eds), *German neo-liberals and the Social Market Economy*, Macmillan, London, 1989.

Peltzman, G., "Toward a more general Theory of Regulation", *Journal of Law and Economics*, 2/76.

Pernice, L., "Multilevel constitutionalism and the Treaty of Amsterdam: European Constitution making revisited", *Common Market Law Review*, 36/99.

Pontifical Council for Justice and Peace, *"Towards reforming the international financial and monetary systems in the context of the global public authority"*, Vatican City, 2011.

Porter, M.E., *Competitive advantage*, Free Press, New York, 1985.

Posner, M., Woolf, G., *Italian Public Enterprises*, Longman, London, 1967.

Praussello, F., "Flaws in the Design of EMU: the Role of Asymmetric Shocks of Federal and National Origin", *The European Union Review*, 3/10.

Preda, D., "First attempts to found an European Federal State: a retrospective glance", *The European Union Review*, 1/99.

Preda, D., *Storia di una speranza. La battaglia per la CED e la federazione europea*, Jaca Book, Milan, 1990.

Prigogine, I., *Le leggi del caos*, ed. it. Laterza, Bari, 1993.

Primavera, S., "Innovazione industriale e prospettive di integrazione nel settore della difesa: verso un mercato UE-USA?", Jean Monnet Interregional Centre of Excellence, Pavia, 2010.

Primavera, S., "L'esperienza americana delle Federal Government Corporations. Spunti di riflessione per la grande impresa federale europea", in Velo, D. (edited by), *L'Europa dei progetti*, Giuffrè, Milan, 2007.

Quadrio Curzio, A., *Economisti ed economia per un'Italia europea: paradigmi tra il XVIII e il XX secolo*, Il Mulino, Bologna, 2007.

Quadrio Curzio, A., *Sussidiarietà e sviluppo. Paradigmi per l'Europa e per l'Italia*, Vita e Pensiero, Milano, 2003.

Rathenau, W., *L'economia nuova*, ed. it. Einaudi, Turin, 1976.

Rathenau, W., *La triple dévolution*, Paris, 1921.

Rideau, J., *Union Européenne. Commentaire des Traités modifiés par le Traité de Nice*, LGDJ, Paris, 2001.

Robbins, L., *Il federalismo e l'ordine economico internazionale*, ed. it. Il Mulino, Bologna, 1985.

Romasco, A.U., *Roosevelt's New Deal. The Politics of Recovery*, Oxford University Press, Oxford, 1983.

Röpke, W., "Wirtschaftssystem und internationale ordnung", in AA.VV., *Scritti di sociologia e politica in onore di Luigi Sturzo*, Zanichelli, Bologna, 1954.

Röpke, W., *Civitas humana. I problemi fondamentali di una riforma sociale ed economica*, ed. it. Rizzoli, Milan, 1947.

Röpke, W., *La crisi del nostro tempo*, ed. it. Einaudi, Turin, 1946.

Rosenstein-Rodan, P.N., *Programming in Theory and Italian Practice*, MIT, Boston, 1955.

Rosenstein-Rodan, P.N., *The Objective of United States Economic Assistance Programs*, MIT, Boston, 1957.

Rossi, G. (edited by), *L'impresa europea di interesse generale*, Giuffrè, Milan, 2006.

Rullani, E., "Pasquale Saraceno: un industrialista al servizio della politica di sviluppo", *Nuova Fase. Quaderni di cultura e politica sociale*, 2/95.

Saraceno, P., *Iniziativa privata e azione pubblica nei piani di sviluppo economico*, Giuffrè, Milan, 1959.

Saraceno, P., *Il sistema delle imprese a partecipazione statale nell'esperienza italiana*, Giuffrè, Milan, 1975.

Saraceno, P., “L’industrializzazione italiana: un processo che non ha precedenti nell’esperienza del mondo occidentale”, in *Economia e Politica Industriale*, 8/88.

Savinio, A., *Scritti dispersi*, Adelphi, Milan, 2004.

Schlesinger, A.M., *The coming of the New Deal*, Houghton Mifflin, Boston, 1959.

Shonfield, A., *Il capitalismo moderno. Mutamenti nei rapporti tra potere pubblico e privato*, ed. it. ETAS Kompass, Milan, 1967.

Sironi Mariotti, M., *Banca Europea per gli Investimenti. I finanziamenti integrativi*, Istituto di Studi Politici e Amministrativi, Verona, 1982.

Sommariva, A., Tullio, G., *German Macroeconomic History, 1880-1979*, McMillan, London, 1986.

Spaemann, A., *Per la critica dell’utopia politica*, ed. it. Angeli, Milan, 1995.

Spierenburg, D., Poidevin, R., *The History of the High Authority of the European Coal and Steel Community*, Weinfeld and Nicolson, London 1994.

Spinelli, A., Rossi, E., *Il Manifesto di Ventotene*, Guida, Naples, 1982.

Spinelli, A., *Come ho tentato di diventare saggio*, Il Mulino, Bologna, 2006.

Teichova, A., Gourvish, A., Pogany, A. (eds), *Universal Banking in the 20th Century*, Elgar, Aldershot, 1994.

Triffin, R., *Gold and the Dollar Crisis*, Yale University Press, New Haven, 1960.

Tsoukalis, L. (edited by), *The Political Economy of International Money*, Royal Institute of International Affairs, London, 1985.

Usai, G., *L'efficienza nelle organizzazioni*, UTET, Turin, 2000.

Usai, G., *Le organizzazioni nella complessità*, CEDAM, Padova, 2002.

Usai, G., *Le imprese*, Giuffrè, Milan, 2007.

Vaccà, S., "Pasquale Saraceno: studioso di politica industriale", in *Economia e Politica industriale*, 72/91.

Vattimo, G., *La fine della modernità*, Garzanti, Milan, 1985.

Velo, D., *La crisi economica internazionale e l'alternativa europea*, Giuffrè, Milan, 1976.

Velo, D., "Emergence de l'ECU face au dollar dans les relations monétaires internationales", in AA.VV., *Les rélations communautes européennes-Etas Unis*, Economica, Paris, 1987.

Velo, D. (edited by), *L'autonomia della Banca Centrale*, Cacucci, Bari, 1995.

Velo, D., *La grande impresa federale europea. Per una teoria cosmopolitica dell'impresa*, Giuffrè, Milan, 2004.

Velo, D. (edited by), *L'Europa dei progetti*, Giuffrè, Milan, 2007.

Velo D., Velo F., *Ospedali e sviluppo economico*, Angeli, Milan, 2007.

Velo, F., "I piani europei e la ricostruzione delle città italiane nel secondo dopoguerra. Sviluppo sociale, economico, industriale", in AA.VV., *Guerra, monumenti, ricostruzione*, Marsilio, Venice, 2011.

Velo. F., "Fiscal Federalism: from the Gramm-Rudman-Hollings Act to the Atlantic Maastricht Treaty", in *The European Union Review*, 1/10.

Vilain, D., "La réglementation des placements est-elle vraiment contraignante?", in *Revue d'economie financiére*, 11/89.

Wallace, H., Wallace, W. (eds), *Policy making in the European Union*, Oxford University Press, Oxford, 2000.

Weber, M., *Il metodo delle scienze storico-sociali*, ed. it. Einaudi, Turin, 1958.

Weiler, J., Wind, M., *European Constitutionalism beyond the State*, CUP, Cambridge, 2003.

Zamagni, S. (edited by) *Economia, democrazia, istituzioni in una società in trasformazione*, Il Mulino, Bologna, 1997.